HENRIETTA SPENCER-CHURCHILL
CLASSIC INTERIOR DESIGN

HENRIETTA SPENCER-CHURCHILL
CLASSIC INTERIOR DESIGN

USING PERIOD FINISHES IN TODAY'S HOME

RIZZOLI
NEW YORK

First published in the United States of America in 2003 by

Rizzoli International Publications, Inc.

300 Park Avenue South, New York, NY 10010

www.rizzoliusa.com

First published in Great Britain in 2003 by Cico Books

2003 2004 2005 / 10 9 8 7 6 5 4 3 2 1

ISBN 0-8478-2558-2

Library of Congress Control Number: 2003104758

Editor: Alison Wormleighton

Designer: David Fordham

Printed and bound in China

PAGE 1 *A Rococo mirror is surrounded by imposing marble busts.* PAGE 2 *A Neoclassical dining room features matching 18th-century furniture.* PAGE 3 *This detail of a Doric column is taken from the covered walkway on page 6.* PAGE 5 *This Georgian window frame is used as a display area.*

Contents

Introduction 6

Baroque & Queen Anne Style 10–35

Georgian Style 36–67

Colonial Style 68–81

Federal Style 82–97

American Empire Style 98–119

Regency Style 120–147

Victorian Style 148–171

Glossary 172

Acknowledgments 174

Index 176

Introduction

ABOVE AND LEFT *Seen opposite, this stone-columned walkway echoes the classical elegance of Greek and Roman designs, revived in the eighteenth century through Europe and America. History provides a wealth of ideas and solutions to even the most contemporary houses and interiors, whether structural, seen left, or decorative, as in the Rococo-style cherub above, winging his way across a gilded bedroom looking-glass.*

History continues to influence us in our daily lives and in the way in which we choose to design and decorate our houses. Ideas have always been taken from the past and from other countries and their cultures. However, these days the process has become increasingly important, as travelling the world is now easier and more commonplace. Our tastes are undoubtedly influenced initially by our upbringing – familiarity breeds comfort. But as your interests develop in a particular field or a certain direction, it is surprising how your ideas can change.

Take, for example, buying or building your own house. In America this is commonplace. Many people will buy a property not for the house itself but for the plot of land, and inevitably the existing house is torn down and a new one emerges. This has both advantages and disadvantages. By building from scratch, you hope to achieve your ideal layout suitable for your existing lifestyle and for the future. The downside is that your home will be lacking in the character that is inbuilt in old houses. Therefore, from an

architectural point of view it is vital, once you have selected your style, to employ an architect and a designer who can assist you in creating your dream home, to add those authentic details that will define the style and distinguish your home from any other new build.

From my perspective, getting the bones of the house right first is paramount, because with the architectural structure in place everything else will follow. What exactly does this mean? The proportions of the rooms are vital – the height of the ceilings in relation to the size of the rooms, and the size of the windows in relation to the height and size of the room. The layout and how you get from one area to another is obviously fundamental, too, as you don't want to end up with many long, boring corridors. Focal points, architectural features (such as plasterwork, panelling, fireplaces and staircases) and floor and wall finishes will all add to the character. The key is to make sure these details are in keeping with the style of the house. For example, a Tudor-style house would look wrong with large Georgian sash windows and Rococo-style plasterwork, and equally a Palladian-style house would look out of place with small windows and linenfold oak panelling.

The same rule also applies to the furnishings, because just as much thought should be given when buying furniture and accessories. Of course, it is important to buy and live with objects you like. Don't rush out and purchase an expensive piece of furniture just because you like it. Ensure that the size, style and period are correct for wherever you envisage it going. With colours and soft furnishings you can be more adventurous and let your individual style and personality shine, but for added confirmation it is wise to consult experts or read books such as this one to get assurance.

In Britain and Europe, where and what can be built is more limited than in America. As a result, rather than starting from scratch, many have to resort to buying what will never seem ideal because of restrictions such as existing style and layout, planning and building regulations, and budget.

When dealing with old properties the key is to respect the existing inbuilt character and turn it to your advantage. Try to restore architectural features as they were originally. If they have been ripped out by previous owners, replace them as authentically as possible.

Fortunately, there are still many highly skilled craftsmen who are capable of reproducing most architectural features, from a sixteenth-century strapwork plaster ceiling to a mahogany-panelled library or a hand-carved marble fireplace.

The purpose of this book is to help guide you through that process, from selecting the correct style of wall or floor finish to the curtains, furniture and lighting, whether you are building from the foundations up or restoring an existing period house. I hope you will find some inspiration to make the challenge more fun and help you appreciate and enjoy living in the end result.

NOTE: The author and publishers would like to thank the designers and photographers responsible for the beautiful images in this book. For full credits, see page 174.

CHAPTER I

Baroque & Queen Anne Style

LEFT AND ABOVE Rich decoration typified Baroque interiors. Elaborate plasterwork on ceilings and on overdoors, often incorporating painted decoration, was combined with fabric-covered or panelled walls adorned with hand-made tapestries. Elaborately carved giltwood furniture and imported rugs added to the opulence of the room, while candlelight completed the dramatic atmosphere.

Grandiose, palatial, ornate – Baroque style is synonymous with splendour and theatricality. The style originated in Italy and spread around Europe during the seventeenth century, reaching Britain by way of France and Holland. Although what could be called early Baroque appeared around 1625, the full style did not prevail in Britain until the beginning of the Restoration, in 1660. It reached its zenith under William and Mary at the end of the century, evolving into Queen Anne style around 1702.

Baroque interiors were characterized by large-scale, heavy forms; walls lined with wood panelling, beautifully patterned gilded leather panels or richly coloured textiles; and ceilings decorated with ornate plasterwork or with allegorical paintings in jewel colours. Intricate naturalistic woodcarvings were applied to overmantels, panelling, picture frames and other wood surfaces. Curves, ornamentation, silver, gilding, lacquerwork and japanning (imitation lacquer), mirrors and blue-and-white ceramics, both Oriental and Delft, were all used lavishly.

ABOVE *An eclectic mix of panelling, painted and gilded wood furniture, and ethnic fabrics and accessories gives the traditional architecture of this sitting room a contemporary feel.*

RIGHT *With its vaulted ceiling, stone columns and stone fireplace, this living room has a robust feel typical of the Baroque period. The furniture adds comfort to the room while the paintings and accessories make it feel lived in.*

The main rooms of a substantial Baroque home were up a grand staircase on the *piano nobile* ('noble' or principal floor), where the ceilings were higher and the windows larger. On the ground floor, the floors were stone flags, bricks or tiles. At the end of the century, black-and-white marble floors became fashionable. Upstairs on the *piano nobile*, oak floorboards were used. Parquet floors appeared for the first time in wealthy homes during this period. Rush matting was a widely used floorcovering early in the period. Rugs from Turkey, Persia and the Far East, as well as English imitations known as 'turkeywork', were sometimes used on the floor, as well as on tables.

Baroque style gradually evolved into a simpler, slightly more subtle and understated version during the reign of Queen Anne (1702–1714), which continued to be popular for several years after her death. The Queen Anne style prevailed in America from about 1720 till around 1750.

ABOVE *Originally, a hardwood staircase such as this would have been left unpainted but the white provides a suitably stark background against which to display typical Baroque and earlier artefacts.*

RIGHT *A curved staircase with beautifully elegant wrought iron balusters and a brass handrail provides dramatic access to the upstairs of this house.*

Halls and Stairs

By the Baroque period, the staircase was considered an important architectural feature. Grand and theatrical, it rose from the central hall up to the principal rooms and often a galleried landing. Instead of a long straight flight of stairs, short flights linked by landings were arranged around a generous stairwell. Grand staircases might be of stone with ornate wrought iron balustrades, but staircases were more typically made from wood, with extensive carved details on the ends of the treads or along the diagonal beam supporting the balustrade. Balustrades varied from simple flat or turned balusters to elaborately carved and pierced panels, which might be painted and gilded.

LEFT *The walls and ceiling of this dining room have been painted in a combination of trompe l'oeil, faux finishes and murals. The room exudes the richness associated with Baroque.*

ABOVE *Although the furniture is 18th-century in style, the overall effect of this dining room with tapestries inset into the panelling is typically Baroque.*

Walls

The main rooms were usually panelled from floor to ceiling. Initially, the panels were small, but they gradually increased in size through the century, with the sections corresponding to the sections of a classical column. The panelling, or wainscot, which had raised mouldings, was usually oak, walnut or pine. Oak or walnut might be left unpainted, but pine was always painted. This could be in a flat colour or with some sort of pattern; it might be stencilled, or it could be painted to simulate more expensive wood, marble, or even tortoiseshell; and it might also be gilded. In Queen Anne houses, the panelling was often painted in subtle shades of one colour, or it might be waxed or limed (pickled).

LEFT *With its magnificent painted beams and panelling, this baronial dining hall is typical of a Baroque room.*

ABOVE *Beautifully aged wood panelling lends warmth to this study, which is given added richness by the fine pieces of furniture and the paintings and accessories. The simple yet elegant stone fireplace provides a contrasting focal point.*

Intricate hand-carved details added further enrichment to the panelling. Initially this was strapwork (ornamentation resembling interlaced straps), but later carving featured naturalistic decorations such as Grinling Gibbons's carved limewood swags of fruits and flowers. Grained or marbled bolection mouldings were often used as frames.

Patterned gilt leather hangings, tapestries or fabrics such as silk damask were hung on the walls. Sometimes lacquer panels imported from the East were incorporated.

Unpanelled walls were plastered and painted with a whitewash or natural pigment colours and often stencilled. Towards the end of the Baroque period, hand-blocked wall-papers were replacing stencilling, but wallpapers did not become fashionable among the wealthy until the early Georgian period.

RIGHT *Moulded beams are a typically Baroque feature. Covered in plain white plaster, these motifs delicately painted over plain plaster pick out the grid that covers the whole room. With such a decorative ceiling, the room needs no further enhancement from wall or window treatments.*

Ceilings

Apart from the fireplace, the ceiling was the most impressive architectural feature of the grand Baroque room. The suspended plaster ceiling, which had a decorative moulded cornice around the edge, was covered with ornamental plaster mouldings. Early in the Baroque period the decoration often consisted of dense strapwork. This, however, was gradually replaced by a grid structure comprised of deeply moulded beams, with decoration such as *trompe l'oeil* architectural painting within each recessed panel, and plain areas between the panels.

Compartmented, or coffered, plaster ceilings like this had been introduced to Britain by the English architect Inigo Jones, who had travelled extensively in Europe and was inspired by ancient classical architecture. Jones was also responsible for introducing the ornate cove ceilings, in which there is a smooth, concave transition between ceiling and wall, found in some of the most palatial houses.

Towards the end of the Baroque period, Jones's rectilinear compartments were replaced by naturalistic plaster ornament such as garlands of flowers, leaves, fruit and shells surrounding central circles or ovals. Dramatic paintings illustrating classical stories also began to appear on ceilings at about this time.

In contrast, more modest homes, along with the non-public rooms of grand homes, had little more than a flat plaster ceiling with no cornice.

RIGHT *The front door of this hallway is emphasized by the pediment and doorcase. The wood finish of the panelled door provides a warm contrast to the stone walls and creates a focal point.*

RIGHT *This elaborately carved fireplace with its plaster overmantel and frieze is typical of Baroque architectural details. The exposed beams of the ceiling and the panelling and shutters add warmth to the room and provide a nice contrast to the stone walls.*

Doors and Fireplaces

The most eye-catching feature in a grand Baroque room, the fireplace was often surmounted by an ornate overmantel. Whether marble, plasterwork or carved wood, it could include such classical elements as pilasters, a frieze, a pediment and a cornice, as well as a picture frame and perhaps even an inset mirror-glass panel. In small rooms, simpler fireplaces were often set across a corner. Similar in style to overmantels, overdoors were typically used in high-ceilinged rooms to make the doorways seem more in scale. Door surrounds featured classical elements such as pilasters, architraves, friezes and pediments, while the doors were large and often simple, commonly with two panels.

ABOVE LEFT *This pretty arched stone window with leaded lights and window seat surrounded by plants is a good way of dressing up what could otherwise be a cold and austere window.*

ABOVE RIGHT *Imposing full-length sash windows are a feature of the late Baroque.*

RIGHT *The window seat in the bay window of this library provides a perfect light-filled reading area. The roller blinds protect the room from the glare of the sun while the curtains give colour and warmth at night without losing light or space by day.*

Windows

Although lavish bed and wall hangings were a feature of Baroque homes, window curtains were minimal or non-existent at the beginning of the period. Often they were just a single piece of thin fabric hung from a rod with rings. Shutters on the upstairs windows provided privacy in town houses, and mats or window cloths were sometimes hooked onto the windows at night to keep out cold draughts. From the middle of the century, blinds made from white silk or damask, Holland linen or painted Indian calico provided protection against the sun (which was important, as fabric dyes were not colourfast).

By the end of the Baroque period, paired curtains were in use. These hung on both sides of the window rather than on just one side, creating the symmetrical effect so sought after in the Baroque period. The pull-up curtain, usually made from silk, was a major innovation at that time. Flat, shaped pelmets and gathered and festooned valances, trimmed with fringe or tassels, were also introduced. These styles remained fashionable through the Queen Anne period, the hallmark of which was the sliding-sash window, which had been introduced in the latter part of the Baroque era.

ABOVE The oak furniture is perfect in style for this 17th-century cottage dining room with its oak beams. The green walls complement the oak, while the matting on the floor adds to the authenticity.

LEFT A carved and painted wooden bench provides a functional focal point in this entrance hall. The bold orange of the walls sets off the wood of the bench and the door frames while complementing the tiled floor.

Furniture

Baroque furniture was robust, sculptural and heavily ornamented. Bookshelves, display alcoves, cupboards and buffets were often built in, and other pieces were arranged formally around the edge of the room, and then moved when needed. Fashionable pieces were made from walnut and decorated with intricate carving, heavy marquetry and gilt. Typical chairs were high-backed, with caned or upholstered seats. Suites of furniture, including ornately framed mirrors, were made for particular rooms, and as comfort became a priority, the wing chair and other upholstered armchairs were introduced.

Lacquer screens and cabinets were very much in vogue. The most important, and elaborate, piece in the Baroque room was the cabinet on a stand. This was supplanted by the chest of drawers and the tall-boy during the Queen Anne period, by which time furniture had become lighter, more simplified and curvier, with graceful cabriole legs.

ABOVE *A blue printed floral cotton on a painted four-poster bed provides interest without detracting from this light and airy bedroom's original features.*

RIGHT *The bed was always a status symbol and in Baroque times a bed like this would have been the most important piece of furniture in the house.*

Beds

The bed was the single most important piece of furniture and a major status symbol in the Baroque home. It was usually either positioned with the headboard against the wall so the bed projected out into the room, or recessed into an alcove. It might even be raised on a dais or set behind a low balustrade. Important guests were received in the bedchamber, while the most privileged were entertained in the 'closet' or 'cabinet' that led off from the bedchamber. In the grandest homes, a 'bed of state' would be placed at the end of an *enfilade* (a line of interconnecting rooms, with the doors aligned so as to provide an impressive vista and processional route).

ABOVE LEFT *Plain blue fabric on the headboard provides a clean break between the embroidered bedspread and blue printed bed hanging.*

ABOVE RIGHT *Crisp white bedlinen provides a clean contrast to the rich gold embroidered bedspread and cushion adorning this bed. Vintage fabrics can be purchased at specialist textile dealers and made up as required.*

LEFT *Carved, twisted posts and a floral tapestry provide typically Baroque grandeur and comfort.*

Tall and stately, most beds were made of wood, with heavily carved posts. Many had a simple four-poster framework that was completely hidden by the hangings. Some had a gilded cornice at the top, others a splendid canopy, which might be either domed or 'flying' (attached to the ceiling by cords, so that there were no endposts). Daybeds had been introduced by this time, too. Often surmounted by canopies, they were used for receiving guests or relaxing.

Bed hangings could be very sumptuous. Made from expensive, richly coloured fabrics like silk damask and often lined in contrasting colours, they were heavily decorated with ornate trimmings and embroidery, such as crewelwork, ostrich plumes, or artificial flowers made from silk or metal. The bedcovers, too, were richly embroidered, while the sheets were mainly white. Wooden 'bed staves' were used to prevent bedclothes from slipping off in the night.

As the hangings became more and more magnificent, the bed curtains, covers and seat cushions of the bedchamber were decorated *en suite* (all in the same fabric). This concept had been introduced by the influential French designer and architect Daniel Marot, who worked in the English royal palaces during the reign of William and Mary. The *en suite* decoration was planned by an upholsterer, who didn't so much upholster furniture as design an entire room. Very important in Baroque times, he was the forerunner of today's interior designer.

Lighting

Firelight was the main source of artificial light in Baroque houses. In modest or poor homes, this was supplemented with rush lights dipped in fat and, from the end of the period, primitive oil lamps in which the wick floated in whale oil. In wealthier homes, tallow or wax candles were used. With its extensive use of gilding, silver and mirrors, the decoration of grand Baroque homes was designed to make the most of this flickering light, as were the various types of candle holders themselves. Brass, tin or silver candlesticks could be placed on candle-stands, or *torchères*, made from turned

wood, brass, pewter or silver. These were like tall, narrow tables with tripod legs and very small tops. They were placed against the wall along with the chairs and occasional tables. A pair of candle-stands holding candlesticks might be placed on either side of a matching table between two windows, then a mirror known as a pier glass in a matching frame would be hung on the wall above the table to reflect the candlelight. Louis XIV *guéridons* were candle-stands carved to resemble a man or mythological figure carrying a tray. They were named after a vaudeville actor popular in Paris at the time.

Wall sconces were mounted on brass plates or, towards the end of the period, mirror-glass back-plates to reflect the candlelight. Branched overhead chandeliers were made from brass, wrought iron or carved and gilded wood. As pulleys had not yet been introduced, they were hung quite low so that the candles could be lit easily.

ABOVE LEFT *This unusual two-tier chandelier has been cleverly wired to provide subtle light over the dining table, and the coral silk shade gives a softer light.*

ABOVE RIGHT *Many antique candlesticks can be converted to electricity and provide a nice base for a table lamp. A coloured silk pleated shade is more in keeping than a modern white shade.*

LEFT *The colours and textures of fabrics play a large part in adding character and warmth to a room. Here the strong red of the cut-velvet cushion provides a dramatic contrast to the gold velvet on the sofa. Neither, however, detracts from the antique tapestry wall hanging.*

Textiles and Tapestries

ABOVE *Antique fabric used as a tablecloth is in keeping with the overall Baroque style of this room, and the striped velvet, although new, looks as if it has been on the wing chair for decades.*

S umptuous textiles were more and more important in grand Baroque homes, where they provided an alternative to panelling in the most important rooms. Walls were covered with tapestries (both English and imported), leather hangings and expensive woven fabrics including silk damask and velvet in rich colours like crimson, purple or gold. The fabric would often be 'paned', or hung in panels with borders of a contrasting fabric and perhaps also a braid, fringe or other trimming (known as *passementerie*). Daniel Marot (see page 31) introduced *portières*, or door curtains, *en suite* with wall hangings, creating a unified effect all around the room. The first chintz fabrics appeared during this period, imported from India. These brightly coloured block-printed, hand-painted cottons were colourfast and were soon very sought after, being used initially as table carpets and stool covers (and later as curtains, bedcovers and wall hangings).

CHAPTER II

Georgian Style

ABOVE AND LEFT *Architectural features, including grand staircases, pilasters, arches, niches and mouldings on panelling, were widely used in Georgian homes. Most panelling was painted, but today it can be painted in one colour, in various tones to highlight the panels, or it can simply left bare. Many moulds of wrought iron railings are available today if you wish to emulate a Georgian staircase.*

The Georgian period lasted from 1714 till 1811, with early, mid- and late Georgian corresponding broadly to the reigns of George I, II and III. 'Georgian style' actually covers more than one style. For the first half of the period, the prevailing style in Britain was Palladian, based on the classical ideas and works of the Venetian Renaissance architect Andrea Palladio. The English architect Inigo Jones had introduced these to Britain a century earlier, but it was the eighteenth-century architects William Kent, Colen Campbell and Lord Burlington who made the style fashionable. Interiors had a weighty formality and dignity. They began to be very 'architectural', with ancient Roman columns, pilasters, pediments and mouldings, along with classical motifs, used throughout. Rooms were sometimes octagonal, elliptical or circular with domed ceilings.

Around the middle of the century, the atmosphere lightened up considerably as elements of Rococo, a style that had already swept Europe, became the latest craze. The lighthearted exuberance and wit of

ABOVE *This built-in bookcase is perfectly matched to the panelling, which has been painted in two tones of off-white to emphasize the mouldings. The colour sets off the leather-bound books and mahogany furniture.*

RIGHT *In this room, strong architectural features such as stone walls and large arched alcoves have been softened with splashes of colour from textiles and leather-bound books in the custom-made bookcase.*

Rococo were expressed in flowing, sinuous lines and a lavish use of C-scrolls and S-scrolls, shell and rock motifs, and plants. English Rococo was generally confined to decorative items like overmantels, mirrors, brackets, picture frames and chair backs, but two offshoots of Rococo had a major impact. These were the 'Chinese taste', or chinoiserie, and the 'Gothick taste', which were romanticized versions of Oriental and Gothic styles.

During the second half of the century, Neoclassicism was the predominant style in England as well as Europe. This was the 'age of elegance', when interiors, though still based on classicism, were lighter and more elegant than Palladian rooms, with decorative detail reducing the dominance of architectural features. Sometimes this is called Adam style because of the huge influence the architect Robert Adam, along with his brother James, had on English interiors.

ABOVE *This impressive Georgian hall has been split up into two areas with an arch supported by marble columns and pilasters with stone plinths. Marble door surrounds and panelled walls add to the grandeur.*

Halls and Floors

In the early Georgian period, the hall once more became an imposing entrance in grand homes, where the architects had often designed the details of the principal rooms, right down to the furniture and carpet.

The entrance hall was generally stone-flagged, with marble and other elaborate paving in some of the finest homes. Geometric patterns and *trompe l'oeil* effects were particularly fashionable. By the late Georgian era, however, the entrance hall had shrunk again, although some large houses also had an outer vestibule giving entry to it.

Butt-jointed wood floorboards were the most common flooring elsewhere in the house. Although used on the floors of the upper rooms for centuries, they were now deemed acceptable on the *piano nobile*, too. In the early Georgian period the planks were oak or elm and were more than 12 inches (30 centimetres) wide, but by the middle of the century, they were usually fir or pine and 8–10 inches (20–25 centimetres) wide. Grand houses might still have oak boards on the main staircase. All boards were generally scrubbed and left unpolished, although pine or fir might be stained and polished around the edges of the room to frame a rug. Parquet was still being laid, too.

Oriental rugs and French Aubusson and Savonnerie rugs were found in wealthy homes, as well as English turkeywork rugs. Around the middle of the century, the English carpet industry began to develop, with pile and Brussels weave carpets being

ABOVE *Two-colour stone floors were typically laid diagonally like this, making the area look wider. The plain border provides a suitable break where the wall meets the floor.*

41

ABOVE *These flagstones are typical of the floors that were found in Georgian halls, particularly in country houses. To recreate this look, either buy reclaimed old flagstones or use one of the many 'aged' stone products available today.*

woven with intricate classical motifs and floral designs. Produced in narrow strips, they were joined to form wall-to-wall carpeting, with borders attached to follow the edge of the room. Although expensive, these carpets became very fashionable.

Introduced in the early Georgian period, painted canvas floorcloths were used in many rooms, even in relatively grand houses. They might appear in areas subject to heavy traffic such as the entrance hall, the dining room or kitchen, or they could be laid under sideboards or washstands to protect the floorcoverings. The floorcloths were painted to match the carpet, or in a chequerboard, mosaic or other geometric pattern.

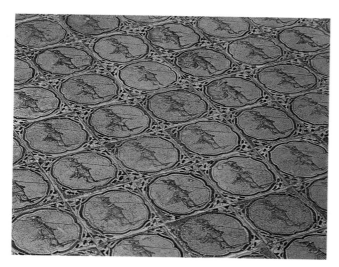

LEFT *Delft tile floors are much more delicate than stone or terracotta floors and should not be used in high-traffic areas.*

ABOVE *Though probably not original, this stone floor is a perfect choice for an entrance hall. If laying a new stone floor, think about the pattern and size of stones in relation to the space, and consider installing underfloor heating beneath it to stop the stone from feeling quite so cold.*

43

ABOVE *The design of this staircase, coupled with the narrow runner, allows the carved tread-ends and the polished wood of the treads and risers to be fully appreciated.*

RIGHT *Early Georgian staircases had turned wooden balusters, as this attractive staircase does. By the late Georgian period, the balusters had mostly become square.*

Stairs

In the early Georgian period, the entrance hall with its staircase became an important feature. Designed to create an impression, it often formed a central well around which the other rooms would be symmetrically placed. The finest houses had stone staircases with ironwork balustrades. On most wooden stairs the handrail was polished and the rest of the wood painted, either in a flat colour or grained. Balusters were now fixed into exposed treads, which allowed the tread-ends to be decorated.

LEFT *The two-toned silk stripe hung on the walls of this Georgian room is typical of the period. It has been finished off with a gilt fillet, often used in grand houses.*

ABOVE *In this elegant drawing room, the moulding and cornice of the floor-to-ceiling wood panelling have been picked out in gilt. The panelling, polished hardwood floorboards, window treatments and furnishings are all sympathetic to the Georgian period, while the carved and gilded wooden pelmets add a touch of Rococo style to the room.*

Walls

Early Georgian, or Palladian, rooms were still fully panelled, but the panelling was usually fir or pine and so was painted. This could be in a flat colour such as muted green, blue, brown or 'drab', or it could be marbled or wood-grained. By the middle of the century, however, panelling only up to the chair rail was preferred. Bold, fairly bulky mouldings were used to create an elaborate cornice at the top of the wall, and a frieze beneath the cornice. Along with the dado (the area beneath the chair rail) and the field (the main part of the wall, above the dado), these sections of the wall corresponded to the sections of a classical column, as they had in the Baroque period.

ABOVE LEFT *The rich patina of the polished hardwood floor and the colour of the walls act as a perfect background to the furniture and paintings in this room, and the white woodwork provides crisp definition.*

ABOVE RIGHT *Despite its narrowness, this entrance hall has been treated as a proper room. The arch with its fanlight frames the view of the staircase nicely.*

LEFT *The tripartite division of this panelling, and the paint finish in one colour, typifies an early Georgian parlour. It was common to paint the cornice to match the ceiling rather than to match the walls.*

Tapestries or luxurious fabrics like brocade, cut velvet, watered silk or damask (or cotton in less grand homes) hung above the panelled dado. The textiles were no longer 'paned' as in the Baroque period, but were edged with a gilded fillet made from cord dipped in gesso, wood, metal, papier mâché or composition. Wallpapers were a slightly less expensive alternative to expensive fabrics and had become very fashionable. Flock papers, Neoclassical wallpapers and hand-painted Chinese papers were all extremely popular.

If not panelled or papered, early Georgian walls were painted with an eggshell paint in vivid colours like crimson, acid green, brilliant blue or pink. By the middle of the century, these had evolved into lighter, matt shades like pea green, sky blue or yellow.

During the late Georgian, or Neoclassical, period the wood panelling gradually disappeared completely. Instead, beneath a wooden chair rail the wall would be plastered and painted in a flat white or stone shade or marbled in a deeper colour. Above the chair rail, it would be plastered and painted or wallpapered. Delicate ornamental plasterwork or bands of carved wood in classical designs were used to decorate the cornice and the frieze, as well as to frame parts of the walls and applied plaster medallions.

Ceilings were high and sometimes domed and/or coffered. One of the major innovations of the late Georgian period was the use of plaster in different tones of a colour within the compartments of a wall or ceiling, with the ornamental plasterwork picked out in gilt. The colours included pale and medium green, lilac, apricot, opal, and stronger blues, greens, pinks and terracotta.

ABOVE *Plasterwork enriches this coffered ceiling typical of the Georgian period. Sometimes the moulding would have been picked out in different colours or gilded.*

RIGHT *This palatial dining room has a curved ceiling and also curved walls with concealed jib doors. Plaster mouldings picked out in gilt emphasize the shape of the ceiling.*

Ceilings

Modest Georgian homes had plain plastered ceilings, but in wealthy homes the ceiling was a key feature. Ornamental plaster mouldings divided these plaster ceilings into formal, symmetrical compartments, often around a central circular section. The mouldings were white, coloured or gilded, and inside some of them might be Neoclassical plasterwork or painted figures or scenes from classical mythology. In rooms designed by Robert Adam, the design of the ceiling might be echoed by that of the floor.

ABOVE LEFT French doors have been treated with lightweight curtains and a swag-and-tail pelmet hanging from a painted wood cornice.

ABOVE RIGHT Venetian windows are difficult to curtain, but this treatment solves the problem without concealing the shape of the window. Other solutions include a swag and tail following the arch; curtains with a shaped, fixed heading; or a rod at the same height as the base of the arch.

RIGHT The silk damask curtains and swagged pelmet on the sash window of this typically Georgian room are the perfect design and proportions for the period.

Windows

Shutters, paired curtains and pull-up curtains were all in use in the Georgian home. The latter was especially well suited to the tall, thin Georgian sash window. If textiles were used on the walls, the window curtains were usually made from the same fabric. In a bedroom the curtains at the windows matched those on the bed. They were usually made from silk, taffeta or cotton chintz and were unlined. As the century progressed, pull-up curtains became fuller and the trimmings more ornate.

The workings of the pull-up curtain were now hidden by a heavy pelmet carved in a scroll shape and either gilded or covered in matching fabric, possibly decorated with appliqué or embroidery. The curvilinear shapes of the mid-Georgian Rococo style were well suited to pelmets, and the furniture designers Thomas Chippendale and Thomas Sheraton designed carved wooden pelmets that often had curved ends and were decorated with scrolls, vases of fruit and flowers, and swags of leaves.

Pelmets gradually became softer-looking and more elaborate, eventually taking the form of shallow swags with small tails (cascades) and 'bells'. By the late Georgian period this Neoclassical drapery was the preferred window treatment.

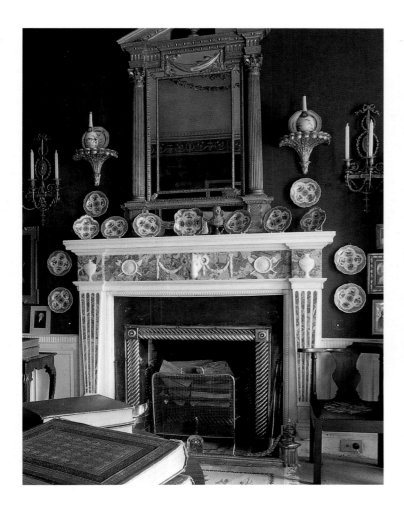

ABOVE *This marble fireplace, carved with leaves and scrolls, reflects classical Greek and Roman influences in its motifs and the symmetry of the design. The fireplace pediment can often be used as inspiration for pediments over doors and bookshelves.*

ABOVE *Different shades of marble create the ornate, but elegant, effect in this elaborate fireplace. Classical features include the columns, urns and swags, while the symmetry of the design allows the rest of the room to be designed easily around this central point.*

LEFT *This stone chimneypiece is French and the style is not found in many British or American homes, although suitable for country houses. The interior is lined with small, attractive French firebricks. The recessed panel above could be used to house a picture or mirror.*

Fireplaces

Early Georgian fire surrounds reflected the sense of dignity of Palladian style. The finest were of carved white marble, often with inlays of different-coloured marbles, but scagliola (imitation marble) and marbled or flat-painted and gilded wood fire surrounds were also popular. The design reflected classical architecture, with carved columns or pilasters supporting a lintel with a decorated frieze, and many had a pediment echoing the pediments over the doors in the room. Elaborate carved overmantels were still in use, often incorporating a mirror, picture panel or sculpted relief ornament. By late Georgian times, fire surrounds had become lighter, simpler and more refined, with shallower relief decoration. Painted wood, scagliola and stone were increasingly used.

The ornamentation changed through the century. Caryatids (female figures), busts on columns, and mask-and-swag motifs were common on Palladian fire surrounds in the early Georgian period. Rococo swirls or Gothic pointed arches often featured on mid-Georgian examples; and Wedgwood medallions, swags, urns and other Neoclassical motifs were popular in the late Georgian period.

RIGHT *This grand composition makes a dramatic focal point in this hallway. A mirror needs to be anchored by using a piece of furniture below it, as shown by the French commode and pair of busts flanking a Rococo mirror. The commode could arguably have been larger for the scale of the mirror.*

ABOVE *Mirrors were used frequently above fireplaces in Georgian times. Here a chandelier lit by candles is hung directly in front of it, allowing the mirror to reflect soft candlelight around the room. In the Georgian era this device was practical as well as flattering to the house owners and their guests.*

Mirrors

Mirrors featured prominently in the Georgian period, not only set into overmantels and in the back-plates of wall sconces, but also on walls. Robert Adam deemed them so important that he designed the mirrors for a room along with the wall and ceiling mouldings, furniture and carpet. Frequently, a tall pier glass was placed between a pair of sash windows, and beneath it was a pier table or console table. On this sat a candelabra, the light from which was reflected in the mirror.

Early Georgian, Palladian-style pier glasses – usually of walnut that might be gilded or painted cream – were very architectural, with pedimented columns. Mid-Georgian mirrors often displayed the Rococo influence, with scallops, shells, palm fronds, scrolls, filigree, even Chinese pagodas featuring in the decoration. Thomas Chippendale was famous for his carved giltwood mirrors of that time. Late Georgian mirrors incorporated classical motifs such as vases, baskets and wreaths.

LEFT *Framed pictures were an intrinsic part of the Georgian interior. They complete a room and add a personal touch, even in small spaces such as this narrow corridor. Make sure that the background colour or pattern does not detract from the pictures.*

Pictures

The Grand Tour that was deemed an essential part of every wealthy young Englishman's education in the eighteenth century ensured that grand Georgian homes were well endowed with pictures. Gilt-framed landscapes and portraits were hung on the walls and above mantelpieces. Georgian overmantels often featured panels in which paintings were inset, and Robert Adam introduced the idea of framing paintings within stucco panels in the room. Sometimes the design of entire rooms was planned to display these trophies of the Grand Tour to best effect.

The Georgian period was the time when miniature painting was at its most popular. Collections of framed miniatures were displayed in cabinets or hung in groups on the walls. It was also the golden age of engravings, etchings and aquatints. These prints were often framed, but another way of displaying them was to glue them to the wall and surround them with printed borders, and *trompe l'oeil* bows, chains and nails. This was done in sitting rooms, studies and dressing rooms, and also in special 'print rooms'.

ABOVE *There is no hard-and-fast rule as to the way in which you should hang pictures, and it is quite acceptable to mix oils with watercolours or prints as seen here. I always think a large picture looks better if anchored by a piece of furniture below it.*

ABOVE LEFT *The growing popularity of book collections promoted the fashion for bookcases, seen here in mahogany.*

ABOVE RIGHT *Mahogany furniture was a feature of the Georgian dining room; here, delicately-turned chairbacks offset the solidity of the long dining table.*

LEFT *The Georgians strove to ensure that furniture was in keeping with the period of the house and the style of the rooms, as in this library with its antique mahogany pedestal desk, pine panelling and mahogany door.*

Furniture

The Georgian period was the golden age of cabinetmaking. The Palladian furniture of the early Georgian period was massive, rigid and restrained, incorporating classical architectural details like columns, pediments and cornices. It was still arranged formally around the edge of a room. Much of the furniture was heavily carved and gilded, with walnut the principal wood. Characteristic pieces include bureau-bookcases, console tables and gilt or white-painted side tables. Chair backs were now much lower, and cabriole legs predominated, most often with ball-and-claw feet.

Mahogany replaced walnut during the mid-Georgian period, particularly for large pieces of furniture. Lacquer was also used for cabinets, screens, tables and chairs. Designers' pattern books, such as Thomas Chippendale's *Director*, were full of fanciful designs for furniture inspired by Rococo style and the Chinese and Gothick tastes. Chinese-inspired chairs and tables could incorporate fretwork, latticework and simulated bamboo, while

ABOVE *A writing table flanked by hall chairs makes a pretty focal point in this hall, with the mahogany lending contrast and weight to the pretty pale blue walls.*

RIGHT *This gilded Gainsborough armchair is suitably covered in a typically Georgian blue damask fabric. It is perfectly acceptable to have a combination of painted, gilded and wood furniture in the same room.*

Gothick taste designs could consist of pointed arches, quatrefoils, pinnacles and crockets grafted onto conventional Georgian cabinets, bookcases and chairs.

Chippendale also designed some fine Neoclassical furniture, but George Hepplewhite and Thomas Sheraton were more closely associated with this late Georgian style. By this time furniture had become plainer and more delicate. Legs were square and tapered or reeded. Satinwood – sometimes decorated with marquetry and inlay – was now widely used, with mahogany in the dining room, and a lot of furniture was painted in delicate, matt colours, often gilded. Upholstery was still *en suite* with other textiles in the room. Typical late Georgian pieces include commodes, a variety of small tables such as tea tables, folding tables and card tables, sideboards and the French *fauteuil* with its padded seat, back and arms. Scagliola panels and Wedgwood medallions were sometimes inset into furniture, and some pieces were ornamented with panels of painted flowers, cupids or mythological scenes.

ABOVE LEFT *This four-poster bed is late Georgian; the cornice is matched at the window.*

ABOVE RIGHT *This pretty bedroom has blue toile de Jouy fabric on the walls as well as the bed, very typical of an 18th-century bedroom both in France and England.*

RIGHT *A floral printed chintz has been used in this country bedroom, with a cotton ticking for the lining. These fabrics are very suitable for Georgian bedrooms.*

Beds

Georgian bed hangings were lighter, simpler and more elegant than in the Baroque period. Four-posters, also known as full testers, remained in vogue until around the middle of the century, when they were supplanted by half-testers. Gradually cabinetmakers, carvers, gilders and painters took responsibility for beds away from the upholsterers, with the hangings diminishing in importance. By late Georgian times, one of the main features of a bed was an elaborate cornice, often repeated above the windows.

Although velvet hangings with gold fringing remained in use, lightweight hangings such as Indian cotton chintzes were increasingly common. The Rococo influence led to lavish, frothy cotton or silk hangings. The 'Chinese taste' was deemed especially suitable for bedroom schemes, with hangings made from Chinese silks or fabrics embroidered with Oriental motifs. Late Georgian bed hangings were formal yet opulent, and decorated with classical motifs and wonderful trimmings. Toile de Jouy – cotton printed in monochrome with engravings of classical scenes – was particularly fashionable.

ABOVE *A combination of electric and candlelight is used in this elegant dining room, and the mirrors reflect the light from both.*

ABOVE *Inspired by delicate chinoiserie fashions from the East, this fanciful ceiling light literally encloses a songbird in a gilded cage.*

LEFT *This beautiful crystal chandelier is perfect for many Georgian rooms whether in the drawing room or dining room or, as seen here, on a stairwell. Many of these chandeliers are now wired, but they would originally have been lit by candlelight.*

Lighting

Lighting was a sign of wealth and status. Even though it was still only candlelight, the amount of candles that were burned increased in most houses, so homes were now much brighter. Silver, wood or glass candlesticks and candelabra were placed on candle-stands in the corners of rooms, and on tables in front of mirrors. In the second half of the century, elaborate candelabra made of silver or ormolu (gilt-bronze) became increasingly prevalent.

In a grand room, a central chandelier of wood, silver, brass or glass with glass drops and chains would hang just above head height, and its candles would be lit on special occasions. Pairs of brass or giltwood sconces were fitted to walls and overmantels. Hanging candle lanterns were used in hallways and stairs, while oil lamps were occasionally used in hallways but were otherwise banished to outdoors.

In the latter part of the eighteenth century, the Argand oil lamp was invented, which increased illumination tenfold and produced no smoke. Families and friends were now able to enjoy communal activities such as card-playing in the evening, gathered around a circular table lit by an Argand lamp.

CHAPTER III

Colonial Style

ABOVE AND LEFT *Shuttered windows, wooden floors and plain walls were typical of the Colonial period and can be used to recreate a Colonial-style home today. Rustic wooden furniture such as the Windsor chair and half-moon table pictured above add to the effect. In America, the backs of Windsor chairs consisted entirely of spindles, with no central splats.*

America's Colonial period extended from the arrival of the first settlers, at the beginning of the seventeenth century, till the Declaration of Independence in 1776. The country of origin of the settlers influenced regional styles, but the local conditions and materials, especially the prevalence of timber, and the particular skills of the settlers meant that a unique style had evolved by the mid-eighteenth century. Styles that were popular in Europe, especially England, began to make their way across the Atlantic in the eighteenth century, though with a time lag of two or three decades, but these, too, were interpreted differently in the New World. Mid-eighteenth-century domestic architecture and interior layouts were classical, based on Baroque, Queen Anne and Palladian designs, but most Colonial homes, apart from the brick or stone mansions of the South, were built in timber.

Wood dominated the interior, from panelling, floors and stairs to fire surrounds, doors and furniture, and the rooms were cosy and increasingly comfortable. Many of the furnishings, including textiles,

ABOVE *This sunny breakfast room has been treated very simply, with no fussy window treatments to detract from the garden view. The wooden beams and country furniture add to the rustic feel.*

RIGHT *Many Colonial staircases were similar to this simple wooden staircase. Known as box winders, the narrow, winding stairs were squeezed in next to the chimney in the centre of the house.*

furniture, pottery and paintings, were made locally, often featuring folk art decoration. Patchwork quilts and embroidered samplers added colour and pattern, while lighting was mainly supplied by candles placed in brass, pewter or wooden candlesticks, iron wall sconces and, occasionally, wrought iron chandeliers. Rush lights and primitive oil lamps were also used.

Shaker style is often regarded as a variant of Colonial style. The Shakers, a Quaker sect from England who initially settled in New York in the 1770s and were at their most populous a century and a half later, believed that interiors should be simple, orderly and functional. Clutter was banished to cupboards, while chairs, clocks, candle holders, baskets, tools and other household items were hung out of the way on peg rails that ran around the walls, roughly at picture-rail height. Probably the best known of all Shaker innovations are their oval or round pantry boxes, which can be stacked in graduated sizes.

ABOVE *The exposed oak plank floor in this working studio is typical of the eighteenth century and adds to the rustic, masculine feel of the studio.*

RIGHT *The beauty of natural wood is allowed to shine out in the wonderful expanse of waxed wooden floorboards in this spacious Shaker hallway.*

Walls and Floors

Walls were fully panelled in the South, but in the North full panelling had been replaced by the middle of the eighteenth century with a panelled dado, or a chair rail and no panelling. Sometimes only the fireplace wall was panelled. Unless the panelling was of the finest wood, it was painted or given a special finish such as graining or marbling. Plaster walls were painted and sometimes stencilled. Imported block-printed or flocked wallpapers were sometimes used in the main rooms. Most houses had pine plank floorboards, which might be painted in a chequerboard design, stencilled, or covered with painted floorcloths or with braided or hooked rag rugs.

ABOVE *This dining room has a lovely early 18th-century feel to it, enhanced by the exposed ceiling beams and horizontal wood-panelled walls and wood floor. The white-painted walls and ceiling between the beams add to the authenticity.*

Ceilings

Early Colonial houses had low ceilings with exposed beams and joists, which either were left untreated or were whitewashed. In the humblest rooms the beams and joists could be quite rough and unfinished, possibly even with the bark left on, but in better homes the beams were properly planed into a square profile. By the end of the

seventeenth century, however, lath-and-plaster ceilings had been introduced, which meant that the beams and joists were completely concealed. These were most often limewashed white or off-white.

More elaborate, moulded plaster ceilings were used in some late eighteenth-century interiors. Based on German Baroque ceilings, they were probably the handiwork of German craftsmen who had settled in Pennsylvania. There were also some ceilings with low-relief ornamentation in the Rococo style, which had become fashionable in Philadelphia and other urban centres of the Middle Atlantic colonies during the 1760s.

Fireplaces

Because logs, rather than coal, were the main fuel in America, seventeenth-century fireplace openings were wide. And as wood was plentiful, it was the most common material for fire surrounds. These were generally fairly plain, often consisting simply of a heavy bolection moulding, with no mantelshelf.

By the early 1700s, the fireplace had become the principal architectural feature of the house. During that century the opening became smaller and the surrounds more elaborate, with pilasters, mouldings or carvings. Marble, brick or Delft tiles were often used for the inner surround.

Overmantels became important, treated as a single entity with the mantelpiece, and surmounted with a broken pediment, which probably matched a pediment that was part of the overdoor. As an alternative to an overmantel, a painting might be hung above the fireplace or even painted directly onto the central panel.

Wood-burning cast-iron stoves such as the Franklin stove (named after its designer, Benjamin Franklin) were introduced in the late 1700s.

ABOVE AND RIGHT *The wood-panelled window cases in this room are beautiful architectural features and make the windows integral parts of the room. Curtains or blinds would simply detract from handsome windows like this. In rooms such as hall or stairs where privacy is not an issue, it is often worth considering leaving windows untreated.*

Windows

Because houses had internal and/or external shutters, curtains were fairly rudimentary in the seventeenth century. Textiles were homespun, such as linsey-wolsey, woven from wool and linen. Wealthy southern plantation houses, however, might boast imported damask or velvet curtains, and by the eighteenth century homespun textiles were being supplemented with other luxury weaves. Printed cottons and chintz were also imported. Toiles, fabrics printed in a single colour with classical scenes, were imported from the 1760s, including some designs – principally patriotic ones – produced especially for the American market. Draperies were more elaborate, and the grandest houses might have pull-up curtains or swags, but they were not generally as lavish as in Europe.

Furniture

Early Colonial furniture was simple and sparse, comprising mainly crude copies of styles that had been prevalent in the craftsmen's mother countries. By the eighteenth century, wealthy homes were furnished with sophisticated mahogany pieces copied from European pattern books, especially Chippendale's, while more modest homes had simple but well-made rustic pieces such as settles, rockers, and wooden chairs. The country pieces were often painted or decorated with naive or folk-art motifs.

ABOVE AND LEFT *Built-in furniture was widely used in Colonial homes and also by the Shakers, whose exceptionally fine cabinetmaking skills produced fine wooden cupboards and ladder-back chairs like these.*

CHAPTER IV

Federal Style

ABOVE AND LEFT *Federal style can provide the basis for a scheme that is cosy and intimate or relatively grand, depending upon the room's architectural features. As the focal point of the room, the fireplace can have a large painting or mirror over it. Overmantels often included a panel for this, but the overmantel, which may feature impressive plasterwork decoration, may be striking enough on its own.*

Named after America's first political party, the Federalist party, the Federal style-period covers the early years of the new republic, from 1776 until about 1820. Lighter and more elegant than the Colonial style that preceded it, Federal style was characterized by symmetry, refinement, grace and restraint. It was based mainly on Britain's Neoclassical style of the Georgian period. As in Britain, rooms were sometimes circular, elliptical or octagonal in shape and were generally more spacious and airy than previously. However, Federal style was simpler, purer and less ornate than the British Neoclassical style. In particular, there was less ornamentation in the form of gilding, stucco and marble. America's third president, Thomas Jefferson, favoured the simplest classical forms, using them in the design of his Virginia home, Monticello, which had a great influence on the Federal style.

The decoration included simplified ancient Greek and Roman motifs, such as scrolling foliage, wheat-sheaves, cornucopias, festoons, urns, lyres, wreaths and columns, and also patriotic American motifs.

ABOVE *The chair rail and simple swags at the windows in this pretty upstairs parlour are in keeping with the period, while the wallpaper is similar in style to those being produced at that time with Eastern influence.*

RIGHT *Wooden floors and wall treatments in pastels, here yellow and blue, reveal the Federal roots of this airy hallway, which has since been decorated with nineteenth-century ornaments and portraits.*

A favourite was the bald eagle, which figured on the new republic's Great Seal – it appeared on everything from fire surrounds and pelmets to mirrors and tea services.

A subtle palette of pastel colours was used in Federal interiors, which, combined with the light, graceful lines of the furniture, created an atmosphere of elegance and refinement. This was further enhanced by the lighting, which came from candlelight reflected off the glass drops of chandeliers and candelabras with engraved glass shades.

The plank floors had not changed from the Colonial era, and might be painted in a solid colour or a chequerboard pattern. However, there was now a better selection of floorcoverings, ranging from straw matting to wall-to-wall carpets decorated with geometrically arranged classical motifs. Painted floorcloths were still widely used, sometimes on top of carpets to protect them.

ABOVE *The curved handrail on this staircase is mahogany, the usual material in Federal houses. Twisted balusters were still widely used at this time, and it was common for the balusters to be in three styles on one tread.*

RIGHT *A fine arch with pilasters and a carved centre keystone frames the staircase and corridor. On the walls is a chinoiserie wallpaper above a panelled dado. The stair runner is held in place with brass stair rods.*

Halls and Stairs

In the finest Federal homes, a spacious entrance hall with its staircase leading up to the main floor was designed to impress. Sweeping circular or elliptical wooden staircases with mahogany balustrades were often built in these houses. The floors in these grand entrance halls might be white marble, or a chequerboard pattern of marble and stone. In humbler homes the floor of the entrance hall was likely to be flagstones, and the staircase straight, quarter-turn or dog-leg in construction. 'Flying', or cantilevered, stairs, in which the inner edge has no means of support, had been introduced but were not widespread. Twisted balusters were popular till the end of the eighteenth century, when they were replaced by plain, square-sectioned balusters, and simpler tread-ends.

ABOVE *This attractive circular room with a domed ceiling is adorned with Neoclassical plasterwork. The walls and insides of the arched niches have been painted in a faux marble finish and enhanced with hand-painted classical motifs. The window treatments are simple and sheer to avoid detracting from the rest of the room.*

Walls and Ceilings

Walls were now given more architectural detail such as arches, pilasters and mouldings. Panelling was generally restricted to the dado and the fireplace wall. Woodwork was grained or painted in an intense 'Williamsburg' blue or 'Federal' green, or a muted colour like grey, deep violet or mustard. The walls were pale – painted and possibly stencilled, or wallpapered in a classical or 'architectural' design. French scenic papers (see page 128) were very sought after. Many ceilings had a central plaster rose, but others were painted in a strong colour, with Adam-style stucco ornamentation picked out in white or gilt.

ABOVE *Half-height panelling divides the walls of this dining room, and the panelling, in turn, has been divided into two sections by the chair rail. The compartmented ceiling is painted in one colour (rather than the mouldings being picked out in a different colour, which is typical of the period).*

RIGHT *This dining parlour shows a typical wall treatment of the period, with plain walls below the chair rail and wallpaper above. At this time many wallpapers were being produced, so they became affordable and more widely used. The mahogany furniture is also typical of the Federal period.*

LEFT *A large fireplace with elegant carving and a panel above the mantelshelf creates a striking focal point in this room.*

ABOVE *This pretty fireplace has the typical swags, urn and medallion detail of the Neoclassical period.*

Fireplaces

Pattern books featuring Adam-style designs were the inspiration behind the Neoclassical fire surrounds that became fashionable in Federal interiors. Painted wood surrounds were the most common, though imported marble surrounds were found in some wealthy homes. A typical design would comprise reeded pilasters supporting an entablature with dentil mouldings. The surrounds were frequently decorated with classical motifs such as urns, swags, fans and mythological scenes, applied as composition mouldings. Fire surrounds were often designed to match door surrounds, dado panelling and cornices. Overmantels were still sometimes used, again with Neoclassical elements.

ABOVE *The windows of this Federal house have fine proportions and in this room the deep recesses provide perfect space for built-in window seats with panelled sides and backs. The panelling is also repeated in the shutters and dado panelling.*

LEFT *The landing of this Federal house acts as an upper hall. The large arched window with a strong architectural frame provides not just a focal point but also ample daylight up and down the stairs. The wooden floor has a painted finish, which also adds to the light and airy effect.*

Windows

As the swag was a Neoclassical motif in itself, swagged fabric was the perfect adornment for the Federal window. Restrained and rather formal, a swag could be draped elegantly over the top of the window, and used either on its own or with curtains. The window treatments in Federal interiors reflected the Neoclassical treatments popular in Georgian England, which were set out in the pattern books widely available in America. However, because imported fabrics, particularly silks, were expensive, and also because the Federal style favoured greater simplicity than the British version of Neoclassicism, the American interpretations of the designs were not as elaborate as their British prototypes.

Imported luxury weaves like silk damask, brocade, taffeta or satin, in vibrant colours such as yellow, blue, green or crimson, were found in the wealthiest homes. Curtains, if used, could be made from these fabrics, but they were often made from muslin or another fine cotton instead and combined with a swag in a more luxurious fabric. Imported chintz and toile de Jouy were also used.

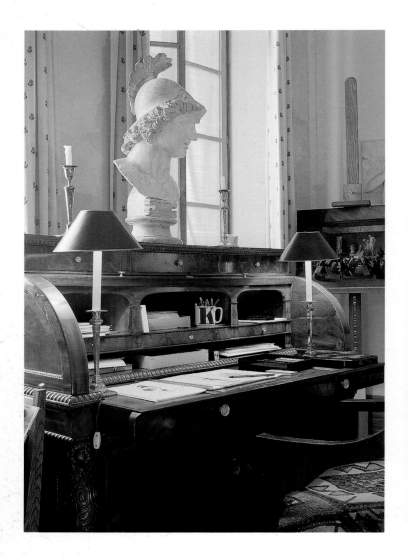

Furniture

Pattern books were the inspiration for furniture, too. Designs by Hepplewhite and Sheraton were more approachable versions of Adam designs, and these were widely used. Because they were freely adapted, with regional variations in the decoration and an intermingling of elements of the designs from different pattern books, the resulting pieces could be very different from the originals.

Federal-style furniture was generally lighter, more rectilinear and more finely carved than Colonial-style furniture. Mahogany was still the most commonly used wood, with light finishes and decorative inlays. Much furniture, however, was painted and often decorated with gilt or japanning. Decoration on the chair backs included landscapes, classical motifs such as lyres, swags and wheatsheaves, and patriotic designs.

The dining room was a Federal period innovation, and new pieces of furniture were introduced for use in it, including the sideboard and extending tables.

ABOVE LEFT *The corner of this room is typical of a gentleman's study furnished with items he may have collected on the Grand Tour of Europe. The roll-top desk is practical as everyday clutter can be concealed.*

ABOVE RIGHT *This chair with its cane seat, back and sides is typical of the period, though the cushions are later. The architectural engravings above it may have been taken from one of the many pattern books of the time.*

RIGHT *A fine marble-topped commode is anchored by a charming group of small paintings with a larger one above.*

LEFT *This wooden bed frame is typical of an American post bed. With its polished wood and white bedspread, it has a fresh, simple feel consistent with the Federal period.*

ABOVE *A four-poster bed, with a cover, skirt and hangings all in a fabric with a striking blue and white botanical motif, provides the focal point in an otherwise simply decorated bedroom.*

Beds

As with furniture and window treatments, pattern books meant that bed designs, such as those by Chippendale and Sheraton, were widely available. Half-testers, which had headposts but no endposts, were now preferred to four-posters. Scalloped bed skirts were widely used at this time. Although velvet hangings with gold fringe were common, bed curtains were generally lighter than previously. Swagged treatments were particularly favoured. Bed curtains made from imported silk were the most luxurious, but block-printed cottons with patterns of birds and flowers, echoing Oriental designs, were also fashionable. They were available in a wide variety of colours. Crewel-embroidered hangings were popular as well. Some bed hangings were made from imported toile fabrics, which depicted classical scenes and were printed in a single colour on an off-white cotton.

CHAPTER V

American Empire Style

ABOVE AND LEFT *Neoclassical decoration, particularly from ancient Rome and Egypt, dominated American Empire interiors, not only in architectural detailing and furniture shapes, but also in wall coverings, textile patterns and accessories. Artefacts like the classical marble dish pictured above were widely used, along with busts and columns similar to those pictured left. Chaises longues and Empire sofas frequently had graceful scroll ends.*

In the 1820s and 1830s, Empire style was the principal fashion in the United States. American Empire was a slightly subdued version of French Empire style, which had been fashionable in Europe since the 1790s and a variant of which appeared in England as Regency style. French Empire interiors were characterized by a lavish use of sumptuous fabrics such as silk in brilliant colours, draped over windows, beds, walls and ceilings. These were combined with massive pieces of furniture decorated with ormolu and gilt. Much of the imagery was designed to extol the glories of Napoleon, whose First Empire in France gave the style its name.

American Empire interiors developed a more robust, opulent look than in the Federal period, with richer decoration, heavier textiles and more imposing furnishings. This was a style of contrasts, redolent of grandeur and luxury. Richly coloured silk, crystal, mahogany, marble, gilt and ormolu dominated the American Empire home. Candles were held in brass, bronze or crystal chandeliers and wall sconces.

ABOVE *This classically inspired hall has a stone floor set in a wooden grid. The symmetrical placement of the furniture gives it the elegant Empire look, and the strategically placed urn adds a focal point.*

RIGHT *With imposing pilasters flanking the double doors, this formal dining room has a strong architectural feel. The beautiful crystal chandelier and torchère add subtle candlelight to the room.*

Architectural fixtures, furniture, carpets, wallpapers, textiles, lighting and ornaments all bore the fashionable decorative motifs – classical ones from ancient Rome and Egypt, along with martial symbols such as crossed swords and arrows, and patriotic American motifs like stars, tobacco leaves, corncobs and the bald eagle. (The eagle was a popular motif in French Empire style, too, because it had been the symbol of the ancient Roman republic and was therefore adopted as a military emblem by Napoleon.)

As Greek Revival exterior architecture became increasingly widespread, in the form of houses built to resemble Greek temples, many interiors reflected the style with a more austere look. The emphasis was on simple elegance and Greek rather than Roman decorative motifs. This look was popular, particularly in the South, in the 1830s and 1840s.

ABOVE *The plasterwork of this country dining room is elegant yet understated, and the walls are not panelled but covered with fabric.*

RIGHT *The panelled wall of this drawing room is enriched with elaborate plasterwork details. The floor is parquet and the furnishings typical of the Empire style.*

Walls and Ceilings

*W*alls were frequently hung with vibrant-coloured fabric, pleated and draped around the walls and from the ceiling to create the look of a military campaign tent. Wallpapers were also the height of fashion, usually combined with floral or architectural wallpaper borders. Some of the papers simulated fabric, while others had a geometric or classical pattern. There was a craze for French 'scenic papers' (see page 128), with special designs being produced for the American market from the 1830s.

Some walls were painted, often with *trompe l'oeil* architectural features such as columns, niches and cornices. Painted *faux* finishes could be combined with architectural

ABOVE *The anteroom of the drawing room on page 103 has very much the same feel, so that the architecture and furnishings flow from one to another. Here, the shutters and panels have been painted with medallions and the cornice highlighted with gilding. The furniture is typical of the Empire period with brass inlay and ormolu embellishments.*

LEFT *In this elegant yet comfortable drawing room, the overall effect is one of European style of the late 18th and early 19th centuries. The door frames, chair rail and dados below have been marbled with the fabric above held in place by a gilt fillet.*

borders mimicking friezes and chair rails, to divide the wall into frieze, field and dado. Stencilling was also used. A popular approach was to use a single strong colour such as crimson, brilliant green or bright yellow for the walls, carpet and textiles.

The walls of a Greek Revival home might have a deep cornice–frieze and a heavily moulded skirting board (baseboard) that marbled or flat-painted wooden, or possibly real marble. The wall between them was wallpapered or painted in a terracotta or stone colour.

Heavily ornamented plaster ceilings with classical motifs within the segments remained fashionable for grand rooms. Also popular were plaster ceiling roses, perhaps combined with a plaster moulding around the perimeter of the ceiling.

Doors and Windows

In American Empire interiors, doors were usually made of pine which was either grained to look like mahogany or flat-painted. They most often had six panels, though in Greek Revival homes they tended to have only two or four panels. Pilasters or columns framed the doorcases, with classical mouldings and classical decoration frequently used on a doorhead or pediment. Sometimes sliding double doors were fitted between the principal reception rooms in Greek Revival homes.

Lavish window treatments provided an exotic contrast to the heaviness and severity of the furniture, with layered drapery replacing pull-ups and paired curtains. Combinations

of heavy and light fabrics in two colours (or three if a contrasting lining was used) were the usual treatment. The lighter material, such as muslin, was used for curtains, while the heavier fabric, such as taffeta, was used for a swagged pelmet and perhaps additional, outer curtains. Many treatments were asymmetrical, with a single curtain draped to one side. In less grand houses, simple white dimity curtains might be topped by a draped shawl to create a similar effect. A roller blind was often used as well.

Curtains and pelmets were adorned with an abundance of fringes, ropes and tassels, with brass ombras to hold them back. Fabric rosettes, which were used to decorate poles, curtains, swags and tiebacks, were themselves an ancient Greek motif. The curtains were hung from brass, gilded, lacquered or painted poles. Often ribbed or reeded, these had ornamental finials and brackets decorated with Empire motifs such as arrows, laurel wreaths or stars.

ABOVE *These double doors surmounted by a carved pediment are in a painted finish on one side of the door and a plain white on the other side, cleverly tying in with the contrasting decorations of the two rooms.*

ABOVE *This white marble fireplace boasts patriotic American eagles atop carved columns that support the mantel and marble figures.*

RIGHT *A dappled fireplace provides the focal point for the layout of this Empire sitting room; the focus is enhanced with a large mirror and draped classical-style vases.*

Fireplaces

Made most often from white, grey or black marble or wood, American Empire fire surrounds were bolder and more austere than during the Federal period. They were not, however, dominant features and so the decoration was relatively plain. Nevertheless, symmetry and proportion were priorities. Fluted pilasters or Ionic or Tuscan columns typically supported an entablature decorated with the Greek key pattern, though often the pattern of the marble provided the only decoration. A slightly raised hearth was common. Overmantels were still in use sometimes, or a framed painting or an oval mirror might be placed on the chimneybreast above the surround.

LEFT *This panelled library, featuring wooden bookshelves with carved columns and inlaid mythological figures, is decorated with ancient stone heads to enhance the classical theme.*

ABOVE *A row of handmade, tooled and gilded calfskin or morocco book spines is the ideal wallcovering for a library; books were often appreciated as decorative objects in themselves.*

Libraries

In keeping with the ideas of civilization and education that characterized the Age of Reason, libraries were a popular addition to the gentleman's home. The continuing vogue for the literary salon, begun in the early eighteenth century as a tea-time gathering, meant that more books were collected. Particularly popular acquisitions were complete sets of the works of Greek and Roman writers such as Virgil and Homer, while the works of contemporary authors were collected by personal subscription. Books themselves were much prized as decorative pieces, and rich bindings that included stamped personal coats of arms were especially made for subscribers' own libraries. Matching, even elegant, sets of bindings with thick gold-embossed Moroccan leather offered wall-to-wall elegance.

ABOVE *This upholstered*
Empire sofa with carved
wood frame and scrolled ends
can be used in all rooms
including at the end of a bed
or across the corner of a
room. The draped leopard
skin adds an electric touch.

Furniture

American Empire furniture was heavier than Federal furniture, with deeper carving and more elaborate decoration. The principal wood was still mahogany, but in a dark reddish shade now. Early in the Empire period, the decoration consisted of applied ormolu (gilt-bronze) mounts, brass and ebony inlay, and gilt. Later, there was an increasing amount of painted, wood-grained or stencilled decoration. In Greek Revival homes, the furniture tended not to have rich carving, ormolu or elaborate decoration.

American Empire furniture was severely rectangular, with shapes and decoration based on classical antiquity. The klismos chair, for example, with its sabre legs, canted back and

curved crest rail, was based on an ancient Greek chair; while the curule chair, with no back and a rounded, x-shaped base, derived from an ancient Roman chair. America's leading cabinetmaker of the time, Duncan Phyfe, was the first to make these chairs in the United States. Figural carving, a typical feature of American Empire furniture, depicted a whole bestiary of ancient motifs, including dolphins, swans, eagles, rams and griffins, as well as mermaids, herms (male deities) and winged caryatids (female figures).

Campaign furniture, such as folding desks, beds, chairs and chests, was very much in vogue. Other characteristic pieces included elegant *chaise longues* and scroll-ended sofas; marble-topped mahogany console tables with gilt swan supports ending in dolphin feet, and with mirrored backs so ladies could check their hemlines; Hitchcock chairs, painted black, with coloured or gilt decoration; and mahogany armchairs, upholstered in brilliantly coloured silk, with sabre legs and sphinx arm supports.

ABOVE *A striking Empire boat-bed, or lit-bateau, in mahogany with ormolu surface-mounted motifs. This can be used as a bed or a sofa and is made more comfortable with the loose back cushions. The French striped fabric coordinates with the curtain fabric. The bedside cabinet is of a similar style and on castors to allow for it to be easily moved.*

Beds

Like the windows, the American Empire beds were heavily draped in layers of vibrant-coloured fabrics. The single beds were placed side-on against the wall, in the French manner. Sumptuous silks or other luxury fabrics, or lavish amounts of muslin, were suspended from a wall-mounted corona and draped over the curved ends of the bed, in a style known as *lit à la turque*. (The hangings were functional as well as decorative, because of the need for protection from cold draughts.) Bolster cushions might be placed at each end of the bed, reinforcing the symmetry of the arrangement.

A new design known as the boat-bed, or *lit-bateau*, was probably the most characteristic style of Empire bed. Named for its shape, and also known as a sleigh bed, it had roll-over or swan's-neck ends. (The swan was a popular Empire theme, because the black swan was the Empress Josephine's emblem.) As with a number of other pieces of

ABOVE LEFT *This pretty four-poster bed with simple hangings is suitable for most country house bedrooms with adequate height.*

ABOVE RIGHT *A metal canopy on this bed allows for the fabric to be draped informally. A fine bobble fringe used to trim the swags is also repeated on the bedspread.*

RIGHT *The feet and headboard of this fine veneered and curved bed are embellished with ormolu.*

ABOVE LEFT AND RIGHT
These two boat-beds both have Empire-style wall drapery, with pictures hung on the backdrop curtain.

LEFT *A half-tester with carved and gilded pelmet hangs over this small double bed which has pretty French blue damask draperies. The frame of the headboard is painted to contrast, while the antique bedspread adds colour as well as warmth.*

Empire furniture, the boat-bed was originally inspired by an ancient Greek piece of furniture, the *kline*. Along with its Roman equivalents, it incorporated plain or carved animal legs, and a headboard and footboard with silver inlay and bronze mounts.

The side-on arrangement of the bed was also deemed to be 'military style'. Continuing the martial theme, silk drapes were sometimes edged with 'campaign' (bell-shaped) fringing, which became fashionable during this period and remained popular throughout the nineteenth century.

Four-poster beds, which had fallen out of favour for the time being, had been replaced by half-tester beds, which had no endposts and in which the canopy was suspended from the ceiling.

Chaises longues were used for relaxing, and also for receiving visitors. Whether they were of the daybed type (with a single end) or the couch type (with two ends but no back, or with one end and a back running only half the width), they were the perfect vehicles for displaying the forms and ornament of ancient Greece, Rome and Egypt.

Ornaments

Classical forms and motifs abounded in the American Empire interior. The walls, carpets, textiles and furniture were covered with classical ornamentation, while griffins, sphinxes, swans' necks and lions' paws supported tables and chairs.

As if that weren't enough, the ornaments themselves were classical in one way or another. Copies in marble, bronze, plaster or Coade stone of Greek and Roman statues, busts and torsos found in the excavations in Italy and Greece were placed on columns or occasional tables. Etruria and Jasper vases by Josiah Wedgwood depicting classical scenes were placed on the mantelpiece, alongside Grecian urns. Also on the mantelpiece could be either an imported French Empire clock with a marble or bronze case embellished with ormolu mounts and classical motifs, or an American shelf clock in mahogany veneer. Above the fireplace would be a *girandole* mirror with an eagle crest (see page 136). Porcelain pitchers, urns and vases that copied classical forms and imagery were also on display, along with American pressed glass in Empire style. On the walls would be framed prints and engravings of classical scenes, and print rooms (see page 59) were still popular in America at this time.

ABOVE LEFT *The base of a table showing a winged lion in a gilded finish. This motif had been used on furniture for many years and was popular throughout the Empire period.*

ABOVE RIGHT *A winged sphinx, here seen as a support for a console table, was used in furniture from the Renaissance period onwards.*

LEFT *These fine ormolu mounts are based on ancient Greek mythological figures.*

CHAPTER VI

Regency Style

ABOVE AND LEFT *Many fine furnishings, from furniture to mirrors and porcelain vases were produced in the Regency era. Mantelshelves became deeper to accommodate the assortment of ornaments being displayed on them. For example, it was common to have a fine clock placed on the mantelpiece along with candelabra which with the help of the mirror above it, added sparkling light to a room.*

*E*nglish Regency style had a boldness and panache that most people find irresistible. Named for the regency of the heir to the throne, the extravagant, dilettante Prince of Wales, the Regency-style period (1811–1837) also covers his reign as George IV and that of his younger brother, William IV. Regency style was the culmination of the classical tradition that had prevailed for over a century in England and Europe, combined with an elegant, modern simplicity. In the Regency interior, there was a strong emphasis on architectural detail and unity. Mouldings were clearly defined, with sharp linear detailing. Ornamentation was principally Graeco-Roman and Egyptian in origin, such as Greek key patterns, swans, crossed spears, winged griffins, sphinxes, palm trees and pyramids. There were also some Chinese and medieval elements as a result of renewed interest in chinoiserie and the 'Gothick taste'.

To complement the stone, plaster and marble of the interiors, soft furnishings became more flamboyant, with a lavish use of fabrics such as rich silks, velvets, taffetas, satins and damasks, along with

ABOVE *Panelling on doors and walls was widespread throughout the 18th and 19th centuries. Here, the wood has been limed (pickled). Wallpaper was mainly limited to the finest houses as it was still scarce and expensive.*

RIGHT *This type of coffered ceiling with intricate plasterwork mouldings was found in grand Regency homes. Often the hallways were two or three storeys high, ensuring that visitors were suitably impressed.*

printed linen, sprigged muslin and cotton chintz. Often in startling colour combinations such as lilac with sulphur yellow, or crimson with emerald green, the swags and furbelows of the window treatments provided a luxurious contrast to the clean, cool classicism of Regency style.

Although the period is known for its exotic tastes – from sabre chair legs and tented ceilings to palm tree columns – most homes were not so flamboyant. Interiors were generally smaller than in the previous century, with lower ceilings, and the furniture was arranged in a more informal way. Lighting was better because of the introduction of cleaner, more efficient oil lamps. Floors were carpeted, upholstery was comfortable, and the general atmosphere was light, airy and elegant.

ABOVE *A fine wooden staircase with turned wooden balusters and a carved handrail forms a striking feature in this hall. The stairs have been close-carpeted but would have originally had a runner fixed with stair rods. Another nice feature is the carved tread-ends.*

Stairs

Staircases became simpler in the Regency period, but they were not neglected, as their value as status symbols was still recognized. In the finest houses, the main staircase was stone, with a mahogany handrail supported on either cast-iron railings (cast iron having largely replaced wrought iron) or plain, square-section wooden balusters, as the fashion for complex shapes of baluster had faded away at the end of the eighteenth century. The handrail of Regency balustrades terminated in a turned bun-shaped cap attached to a slender newel post. Sometimes the newel post was replaced by railings or balusters arranged in a tight circle. The tread-ends were often ornamented with carving.

In less grand homes, and on the upper flights in wealthy homes, the staircases were generally of wood and were much the same as the wooden staircases of the late Georgian period. As on the Georgian stairs, the balusters were fixed into exposed treads, without the diagonal board, or 'string', at the outside hiding the steps; this is known as 'open-string' construction. Any ornamentation was classical and usually consisted of a simple moulding below the 'nosing' (the front edge of the tread) or turned detail on the newel post. Like the stone staircases, wooden staircases usually had a polished mahogany handrail. All the wood of the staircase, apart from the handrail, was generally painted a dull, flat colour or wood-grained. A narrow drugget (a thin carpet runner made of coarse wool) was usually nailed to the wooden steps. Back staircases or flights leading to the attic remained extremely simple and were typically winding or had small landings.

ABOVE *Stair balusters became much simpler in the Regency period. Either wooden or painted or in cast iron, they were uniform throughout, but normally with a polished handrail. The pictures are cleverly hung on chains from a picture rail, which simplifies the hanging process on a stairwell.*

LEFT: *With a stone floor laid on the diagonal and surrounded by a border, this elegant hall is enhanced with the plasterwork medallions and enrichment which are also repeated in the niches and ceiling.*

Walls and Ceilings

As a result of the Regency period's emphasis on form and shape rather than ornament, Regency walls and ceilings in smaller rooms were much plainer than their Georgian equivalents had been. Expanses of plain colour replaced applied mouldings and ornament, with decorative paint effects often used to provide variety. A contrasting stencilled or wallpaper border might also be added.

Where the ceiling was high enough, walls were still usually divided into three main sections – frieze, field and dado – with classical decoration or decorative paint effects such as bronzing or wood-graining on the cornice, chair rail and skirting board (baseboard). The dado was often still panelled in wood, with the wood painted a pale stone shade, and also often given a *faux* stone, marble or wood-grain paint effect. If the dado was not panelled, it was sometimes given *trompe l'oeil* panelling instead.

The field (main part of the wall) might be painted a strong, matt colour such as emerald green, acid yellow, terracotta, deep pink, crimson, maroon, lilac or strong blue and gold. As well as *faux* paint effects, stencilling was often used to add pattern. Or the wall could be covered in a textile – the fabrics that were used ranged from worsted and cotton to damask and taffeta. Wallpaper was another possibility, as it was now more

ABOVE *This fine hall has a limestone floor with slate or marble insets typical of those used throughout the 18th and 19th centuries. The strong cornice provides a break between the walls and coffered ceiling, and the symmetry adds to the Georgian feel.*

widely available than ever. Sophisticated wallpapers that appeared in Regency homes included flocked and moiré-patterned papers, both simulating expensive fabrics, and papers imitating decorative paint effects. Wallpapers with small repeat motifs such as little wreaths or stars were popular, too. Imported hand-painted papers were much sought after and highly fashionable.

The 'Chinese papers' that had been high fashion in the mid-eighteenth century were still being imported and were especially popular for bedrooms. Another, newer type of hand-painted paper, known as 'scenic papers', came from France and was similar in concept, in that the papers were designed to be placed in sequence on all four walls of a room, forming a continuous scenic panorama. Because of their expense, however, they

were often cut into panels instead and 'framed' with paper borders. After the initial success of the hand-painted papers, manufacturers block-printed them.

Ceilings were now usually plain, with only a decorative rose in the centre, from which a chandelier would hang. By contrast, however, 'cloud ceilings', another decorative paint effect, were very popular. With the popularity of lavishly draped fabric came the tented ceiling. Also fashionable in France as part of the Empire style, tenting involved draping pleated fabric over the walls and/or ceiling, often with a draped or shaped pelmet separating the two. Much of the inspiration for Regency decoration came from the British campaigns against Napoleon in North Africa, and tenting was inspired by military campaign tents.

ABOVE *With stark white paintwork used to emphasize the columns and other architectural details, this hallway has a fresh, light feel. The pale blue walls provide a subtle contrast to the painted woodwork and mahogany furniture, providing an updated Regency feel. Originally the floor would have been stone or wood, not wall-to-wall carpet.*

ABOVE *Elegant pull-up curtains are used at the windows of this grand drawing room, which is divided into three sections by Corinthian pilasters and columns enhanced with gilding.*

RIGHT *In this country drawing room, the windows have elegant swags and tails, with the shape following the top of the Venetian arched window.*

Windows

Lavishly dressed windows were one of the hallmarks of Regency style. Inspired by the French Empire style, they consisted of many layers, often arranged asymmetrically, and trimmed with fringes, tassels and applied braid. The outer curtain was frequently left purely as a dress curtain, elegantly draped back and held in place with a rope cord and tassel or an ombras (wood or metal hold-back). The second layer was of silk or muslin and might be drawn to one side only. Most windows also had a blind for privacy and protection against sunlight. Above the window, decorated poles with elaborate finials and brackets were elegantly draped with separate lengths of fabric. When there were two or more windows on one wall, they were linked with continuous drapery.

Doors and Doorways

Tall double doors became common in Regency houses, even relatively modest ones, thereby allowing two interconnecting rooms to function as one. Like other architectural elements of the Regency house, the doors were simpler in design than during the late Georgian period. Regency doors had four or six panels, with thin mouldings delineating the panels. In a grand room the door casing could have an architectural head in a Greek Revival, Egyptian, chinoiserie or Gothick taste.

ABOVE AND LEFT *The interesting pediment over the doorway on the left is a later addition and sits on half-round columns. The painting within the pediment is trompe l'oeil as are the wood-grained sections, repeated in the bookcases. In the same room, the mahogany panelled double doors pictured above are surmounted by a carved and gilded pelmet intended for a curtain pelmet.*

133

Fireplaces and Alcoves

Marble was preferred for Regency fireplaces – usually with carving picked out in gilt, or with inlaid marble – but porphyry was popular, too. Wooden surrounds were painted with a *faux* finish to look like marble, porphyry, bronze or a more expensive wood.

The fireplaces were much simpler, lighter and more austere than Georgian fireplaces. They typically consisted of flat jambs with reeded decoration, supporting a plain lintel surmounted by a mantelshelf. Early in the period, the shelves were narrow, but the variety of objects available to display on them led to a fashion for deeper mantelshelves.

Alcoves provided another good opportunity for displaying antiquities or collections, particularly the alcoves at either side of the fireplace. Most often, china cupboards and bookcases would be built into them.

LEFT *A carved console table with marble top is painted and the mouldings picked out in gilt. Italianate in style, it is the perfect piece for a narrow hallway or corridor. Usually a mirror in matching style would be hung above it.*

Mirrors

Much use was made of mirrors in Regency interiors. Large rectangular chimney-glasses in painted or gilt frames often sat directly on the mantelshelf. The decoration usually consisted of reeding, roundels at the corners, and ancient Greek or Egyptian motifs. The best-known Regency mirror is the *girandole* convex wall mirror. This round mirror had a gilt frame ornamented with balls and possibly a bead moulding around the edge. It might also be crested with an eagle, or have snakes at either side serving as candle sconces.

Mahogany or satinwood cheval mirrors, or standing dressing mirrors, were highly fashionable for the dressing room, making it possible to view a full-length reflection.

RIGHT *This elegant composition of furniture provides a symmetrical and balanced focal point within the room. The furniture is harmonious in style, and the animal carvings also link them together. The walls are covered in fabric to match the curtains.*

ABOVE *An antique library chair covered in leather is perfect for this masculine room. The walls are painted in a soft celadon-coloured rag finish which adds to the feeling of age.*

RIGHT *A group of marble and clay busts and statues forms a wonderful display on an octagonal side table. The lamp and strategically placed mirror add depth to the display.*

ABOVE AND LEFT *This beautiful library has a masculine yet elegant atmosphere, largely created by the custom-made bookcases, with their egg-and-dart moulding. The leather-bound books complete the look.*

Libraries

*H*aving been principally a male domain previously, libraries were now being used by the whole family. Built-in bookcases were virtually essential. They were usually architectural in design, with classical mouldings, cornices, pediments and possibly pilasters. Sometimes they were fitted with glass-panelled doors, as they were also used for displaying collections. Bureau-bookcases were also used, and a new innovation was the revolving bookcase. In addition, as part of the general move towards more comfort and versatility in the library, card tables, canterburies for storing periodicals, and sewing tables appeared. These were mainly made from mahogany or rosewood, but satinwood was favoured for the more delicate pieces. Sofas were now arranged at right angles to the fireplace, and in front was the newly introduced sofa table, which 'the ladies chiefly occupy them to draw, write or read upon', as Thomas Sheraton explained.

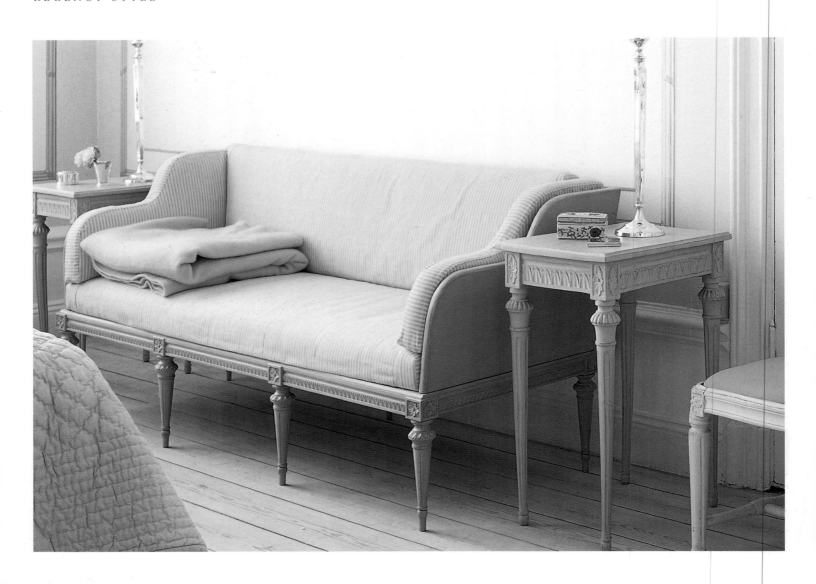

Furniture

Much furniture of this period was based on ancient Greek pieces. Made of mahogany or rosewood, a Regency chair had a low back, on which the top rail curled over backwards, and sabre legs. The seat was caned or upholstered in silk, damask, brocade, linen or cotton. The Grecian sofa (with curved ends, bolsters and carved lion's-paw feet) and the *chaise longue* are among the best known. Along with the revival in chinoiserie, japanning (imitation lacquer) and *faux* bamboo became popular again. Wooden furniture was decorated with inlay and carving, featuring Greek and Egyptian motifs in particular. Occasional tables, sometimes with lyre supports, proliferated. A round table was placed in the centre of the room, with an oil lamp on it, and other pieces were arranged informally around the room, away from the wall.

ABOVE LEFT *A pretty painted Regency-style sofa in a painted finish is upholstered in a ticking fabric. The side tables are in the same style and finish, and they sit well on the pale wood floor.*

LEFT *Detail of a boat-bed which has loose seat and back cushions covered in rich red and green velvets to complement the wood. The fabric is also suitable for the period.*

ABOVE *A gilt Regency sofa with blind cane back and upholstered seat with loose back and seat cushions. These pieces are more sturdy than they look and suitable for use in all rooms, from halls to drawing room to bedrooms.*

RIGHT *A slipcover is used on this pretty serpentine-shaped sofa which is in a chintz with chinoiserie theme typical of the 18th and 19th centuries and still popular today. Slipcovers were also used in the Regency period to protect upholstery in the summer.*

ABOVE *Here a French-inspired boat-bed is given a less frivolous look than the Empire-style boat-beds pictured on page 117, with framed pictures replacing wall drapery.*

RIGHT *This sumptuous four-poster bed has all the posts covered in fabric. Normally the top would have a carved wooden cornice but in this case it has been elaborately cut out and covered. At the end of the bed, the curule chair with its carved animal feet is typical of the early 19th century.*

Beds

Regency bed hangings, like the window treatments, were lavish and multi-layered. The bed, windows and walls of the bedroom were swathed in yards of richly coloured silks, bright-coloured chintzes and diaphanous muslins. Sometimes the swags above the windows continued right around the room, over the door frame and chimney-breast, and around the top of the bed, then the fabric of the bed hangings and windows would also be hung from the walls. Many of the curtains were lined in contrasting colours, increasing the dramatic effect when the curtains were tied back with tasselled cords during the day. Dark green with gold or salmon pink was a typical combination.

Empire style was fashionable in France and Europe at about the same time as the Regency period in England, and beds inspired by Empire style were the height of

LEFT *This fine four-poster has an elaborately carved frame, cornice and posts and thus the end posts have been left untreated while those at the head are probably of plain wood so have been fabric-covered. It is quite common to use a contrasting, plainer fabric to line the inside of the bed curtains and canopy.*

fashion, as they were in America a little later (see pages 114–17). Based on widely available pattern books, these beds were either half-testers or single beds with no framework from which to hang curtains. A bed was placed side-on against the wall, and the drapery hung from a canopy or rod attached to the wall or ceiling, and then draped over the ends of the bed. Empire-inspired 'sofa beds' were treated in a similar way.

The four-poster 'English' bed was less fashionable through the Regency era. Nevertheless, many people still preferred them, dressing them with great elegance. Unlike Empire style, Regency style included Gothic Revival shapes and motifs, and Gothic Revival four-posters were designed, complete with heavy curtains, swagged drapery and gilded cornice with pinnacles and crockets, worthy of the grandest medieval castle.

ABOVE *This bed, rather than having posts, has a suspended tester. The fabric, a silk damask with elaborate scrolling in a contrast fabric, is edged in a silk cut fringe. The shape of headboard has been imaginatively sewn onto the backdrop curtain.*

CHAPTER VII

Victorian Style

ABOVE AND LEFT *Victorian interiors were cosy, warm and inviting, with comfortable upholstered seating and a plethora of textiles. The use of trimmings was at its height during the Victorian era. In the photograph above, a heavy tasselled fringe with braided top is used on the lower edge of the curtains. Wall treatments and furniture were extremely varied because so many style revivals were occurring simultaneously – eclecticism was the norm.*

The Victorian era – the period when Britain's Queen Victoria was on the throne (1837–1901) but the name of which was actually used to describe this era all around the world – was unlike any other in terms of style and interior decoration. It can only be described as an eclectic mix of past styles, freely interpreted and with no single style prevailing. It was not unusual to find a combination of different styles all under one roof – there might have been, say, a Neoclassical hall, a Gothic Revival library, a Neo-Rococo drawing room, a Neo-Elizabethan dining room and a Moorish smoking room. The plethora of style revivals did not occur all at once, of course, and some lasted longer than others. The Gothic Revival was probably the longest-lasting and most widespread.

The Victorians adored colour and pattern, and they crammed their rooms full of it. Reception rooms tended to be decorated in darker colours and with heavier fabrics, while chintzes were reserved for bedrooms. A lot of the furniture was overstuffed, and as much of it was packed into each room as possible.

ABOVE *This timber-clad ceiling is typical of the heavier Victorian look, in which ceilings were panelled or had deep cornices and elaborate mouldings, and were often a dark colour. Here, because the ceiling is high, the wood produces a warm effect without dominating the room.*

RIGHT *Applied panels with a combination of antiqued mirror finish and a tortoiseshell-effect painted finish are used on the walls of this dining room. A similar paint effect is used on the ceiling, which reflects the candlelight and gives the impression of a night sky.*

Any remaining spaces were then filled with accessories. To augment this, houseplants proliferated, and souvenirs of world travels plus other collections were proudly displayed. Windows and furniture were all draped with heavy fabrics, making the rooms seem not only cramped but also dark. Needlework such as *petit point*, embroidery, Berlin woolwork (a type of multicoloured needlepoint worked from printed charts) and beadwork was practised as a hobby, so a variety of throws, cushions, fireplace hangings and screens were also to be found in most rooms.

To a modern eye accustomed to minimalism and open-plan living, the Victorian interior could seem highly claustrophobic and oppressive. But at night, with a blazing fire and mellow lighting by oil lamp (and eventually gaslight), its deep-buttoned sofas would seem very cosy and inviting.

ABOVE A narrow corridor has been cleverly furnished like a room, with the dado and walls above littered with paintings. The commodes break up the long run of wall, and the skylight adds an interesting filter of daylight into a dark space.

Halls and Floors

arpets were laid either wall to wall or with a narrow band of wood floor showing all around, which would be stained, painted or marbled unless it was parquet. Carpets generally had large patterns, such as floral motifs with a geometric border of acanthus leaves or a Gothic pattern. Colours were typically reds, greens, browns and cream. Upstairs, the bedrooms were more likely to have rag rugs or painted floorcloths on top of the floorboards.

Encaustic tiles, inlaid with geometric or heraldic patterns, were fashionable for halls and porches. They were laid in intricate patterns with plain 'geometric' tiles in different shapes and sizes. Ceramic tiles and marble slabs were also often used in halls.

ABOVE *This Victorian billiards room has been influenced by the Gothic Revival style which is repeated not only in the pointed arch of the door frame and other architecture but also in the furniture and billiard accessories. The chequerboard floor pattern runs diagonally in the traditional way, making the room look wider.*

RIGHT *Widely used and very popular, this traditional stone floor with insets of slate or marble is suitable for a range of period-styles and many different rooms, particularly hallways. In the past, the locally available stone would have been used, but today imported limestone is often substituted.*

LEFT *The walls of this dining area have been hand-painted in a trompe l'oeil design. The floor above is visible between the exposed beams and joists of the ceiling.*

ABOVE *The original structure of this room has been left exposed, while the rafters have been plastered over. The ceiling is painted the colour of the walls so they appear to merge.*

Walls and Ceilings

Although the dado was absent from many early Victorian rooms, it reappeared around 1860, when walls were again divided into dado, field and frieze. The dado might be wood-grained or painted a dark colour (possibly on an embossed paper), with a patterned paper used on the field. The frieze might have a different patterned paper, or it could be painted along with the ceiling. There was a huge variety of wallpapers, and stencilling was used as well.

Ceilings varied considerably in design and complexity, but most had some sort of plaster ceiling rose. Anaglypta, a raised, moulded wallpaper, was a popular alternative to plaster. Ceilings were generally painted off-white or stone-coloured.

Fireplaces

The hearth was the centre of family life in the Victorian home. In those days there were still servants to clean the grate and hearth in the morning while the family slept. As a result, there were fireplaces in practically every room, and the fire surround was sometimes even changed when the room was redecorated. Fire surrounds were generally made from marble in various colours, slate (sometimes cunningly painted to make it look like marble), cast iron or fine hardwood such as mahogany or rosewood. Pine was used, too – either flat-painted in a dark colour, marbled or wood-grained to look like an expensive hardwood. The lighter-coloured marbles such as white or grey tended to be reserved for living rooms, while black was preferred for dining rooms and libraries.

The mantelshelf became deeper as the fashion for displaying ornaments and clocks increased, and a huge, framed ornamental mirror was often placed above it. In the late Victorian period, an overmantel incorporating side mirrors, a large central mirror and shelves was typically found in larger rooms.

FAR LEFT *Although predominantly Gothic, this fireplace has the added grandeur of the Baroque. The stone finish looks good against the painted panelling of the walls.*

157

The designs of the fire surrounds were often inspired by one of the historical styles that were enjoying a revival in the Victorian period. Gothic, Renaissance, Baroque or Georgian were the most important styles but fire surrounds in Queen Anne, Rococo, Baronial, Aesthetic, Arts and Crafts and, in America, Colonial and Shingle styles all had their fans as well.

New fire regulations came into force in Britain during the Victorian era. In the new-style, arched, cast iron register grate, the grate, fireback and inner frame were cast as one piece. This type of grate not only lessened the risk of a chimney fire but also allowed the air supply to be controlled with the use of dampers. A few of these register grates were plain, but most were decorated with panels of plain or multicoloured heat-resistant tiles at the sides, which added splashes of colour to the black grate. Some sets of pictorial tiles were designed to form a complete picture when all five were

ABOVE *Although very much part of the panelling, this carved wooden fire surround still forms a focal point in the room. The frieze has a central design, and the polished marble slips (inner surround) are in a bolection moulding rather than being flat.*

placed one above the other. Floral, geometric, Art Nouveau and Delft tiles were among the other styles that were used.

A cheval firescreen was also sometimes used to hide an empty grate. In line with the Victorian mania for covering everything with fabric, heavy draped curtains were sometimes hung around the fireplace, and these could be used to cover it up when not in use. The mantelshelf was often covered with a mantel-valance made from a costly fabric, possibly decorated with embroidery, beadwork, fringing or appliqué. In some instances it was virtually impossible to see the fireplace beneath all the fabric and ornaments.

Alongside the fireplace sat a brass or copper coal scuttle or wooden coal box, and all the other paraphernalia needed to use the fireplace effectively – a fender, bellows, trivets, long-handled brushes and a fire-iron set: shovel, poker and tongs – plus, of course, the pole screen to protect the face of anyone sitting near the fire from direct heat.

ABOVE *On this unusually long dormer window in an attic, a roller blind (shade) has been combined with a stiff, shaped pelmet in the same fabric. The use of two wallpaper patterns emphasizes the angles.*

RIGHT *These stunning Gothic windows are such an architectural feature that it would be a shame to detract from them with curtains, particularly as the walls and floor provide enough pattern.*

Windows

In Victorian interiors, pairs of curtains hung down straight and were tied back at a lower level than in the Regency or Empire periods, using brass or ormolu hold-backs or cords and tassels. Fabrics included heavy silk or worsted damask, figured satin, cut or plain velvets, felt (only in dining rooms), cretonnes (floral prints on cotton, used mainly in bedrooms or as summer curtains) and chintz (again mainly in bedrooms). The colours were much more vivid than previously because synthetic dyes had recently been invented. Deep fringed, tasselled or bobbled braids were heavily used as borders, sometimes with a wide one and a narrow one used alongside each other on the lower edges of curtains. Lace or muslin under-curtains were universal, and most windows also had roller blinds

ABOVE LEFT AND LEFT
Where there is not enough space for curtains, whether in a small room or in a window recess, a simple blind hung from a pole can be the answer. In both the tiny bedroom on the left and the sitting room above, the lack of curtains is offset by a heavy use of other textiles in bed curtains, tablecloths and upholstery, just as the Victorians did.

ABOVE RIGHT *During the Victorian period many different types of fabric were available, from plain and patterned velvets to brocades and damasks or printed chintzes. Often a variety of patterns was used within one room, as pictured here.*

(shades) usually made of Holland linen (a type of canvas). Fringes were often added to the blinds, and sometimes the blinds were painted. Door curtains, known as *portières*, were also typical of many Victorian interiors.

Flat pelmets were in vogue once more, sometimes shaped to reflect the style of the room, such as Gothic Revival or Neoclassical. Pelmet boards could be built out in either a semicircular or a rectangular shape and covered with a goblet-pleated valance, or they might be topped with a giltwood cornice. Some flat pelmets had a shaped outline which continued down the each side of the window. Known as lambrequins, they were combined with symmetrical main curtains and often also an asymmetrical muslin under-curtain. Lambrequins went out of fashion by the end of the Victorian period, however, as they cut out so much light.

In treatments where a flat pelmet or lambrequin would have looked too severe, a draped pelmet or valance in a lightweight fabric was sometimes used. Swags and tails were still fashionable too, particularly on bay windows. Also popular was scarf drapery, in which one piece of fabric was draped elegantly and simply as a heading.

Curtains were hung from thick brass or wooden poles. The wooden ones were sometimes painted gold or wood-grained, embellished with decorative finials and brackets.

LEFT *Oil paintings are mixed with engravings, watercolours and mirrors all on one wall here, but the overall effect is quite acceptable, and the William Morris wallpaper does not detract.*

ABOVE *These black and white engravings look striking on the red walls. Strong colours tend to make a better background for prints than pale washed-out ones do.*

Pictures

Just as an empty bit of floor space would be anathema to the Victorian householder, so every bit of wall space was also there to be put to good use. No Victorian home would have been complete without a lavish display of framed paintings and prints, and during the early Victorian period, in particular, the aim was to cover each wall from dado to cornice with closely packed oil paintings, watercolours and engravings. Highly varnished landscapes, portraits of the occupants of the house in crayon or oils, delicate watercolours of flowers and plants painted by friends and family, and intimate charcoal sketches would all jostle for space with framed sporting prints, which were in their heyday at this time. And if space was short, a prized picture could always be displayed on an elegant decorative easel, made from mahogany, rosewood, real or *faux* bamboo or papier mâché inlaid with mother-of-pearl.

ABOVE *The painted finish prevents these bookcases from dominating the library. I like the gilding on the dentil of the bookcase cornice and the trimming on the shelves.*

RIGHT *In this library an impressive built-in bookcase along the full length of one wall ties in nicely with the existing architecture but still looks like furniture.*

Libraries

Libraries became common features of Victorian houses in Britain and America, and fitted bookcases were built in which to store the books. But although the bookcases were built in and fitted the space exactly, they looked more like free-standing furniture. The traditional breakfront design had a large central section with glass doors, and this projected farther into the room than the open-shelved sections on either side. Often elaborately moulded, the bookcase would be topped by a cornice. Other library furniture included a 'drum' table in which to store paper, a writing desk and comfortable armchairs. Gothic Revival was regarded as a particularly suitable decorating style for the library.

ABOVE *Leather furniture is a good choice for a Victorian-style room, particularly if it has an aged and worn look or buttoning, as seen in the velvet side chair above. When re-covering old sofas and chairs try to retain the original horsehair or replace it with a modern equivalent to keep the same shape.*

Furniture

Because so many styles were revived during the Victorian era, a corresponding number of different styles of furniture appeared. Most of these were not so much exact copies of the originals as pieces inspired by a style.

Furniture in the Victorian house was arranged in conversational groups, and comfort was the main priority. With the introduction of the coiled spring, this meant that upholstery was deep and plump. Shapes were rounded and opulent, and chairs and sofas were often deep-buttoned, until around the 1880s when deep buttoning went out of fashion. Ottomans of all shapes and sizes were to be found in front of fireplaces, while the *chaise longue* and the love seat became familiar sitting room pieces.

Mahogany was the preferred wood for furniture, although oak was used for Gothic and Elizabethan styles. At the end of the Victorian period, when the Queen Anne

revival commenced, the overall look became lighter and walnut or satinwood was used for finer pieces. New furniture found in the sitting room included the 'whatnot' (a tiered stand), which was essential for displaying the vast quantities of bric-a-brac typical of a Victorian room, and the small desk known as a davenport. Circular and oval occasional tables, covered with chenille or velvet, provided yet more surfaces for display. In the dining room, heavily carved, ponderous furniture was preferred. Sideboards were ornate and often had carved backs with over-mirrors. Dining tables, whichever revival styles they were based on, were generally large and could be extended to make them even larger. The most typical dining chair was the balloon-back (which was also made for the sitting room, but with cabriole legs).

The Victorians had a taste for the exotic in their home furnishings. Popular items included tables, chairs, whatnots and other pieces, as well as accessories, in japanned (imitation lacquer) papier mâché with mother-of-pearl or painted decoration. The larger pieces often had a core of wood or metal to make them stronger. Towards the end of the period, wicker furniture also became popular in both Britain and the United States.

ABOVE LEFT *A button-backed 'sociable' double chair allowed two people to talk together comfortably without turning their heads. The deep fringe is typical of the Victorian love for trimmings, and the fabric echoes the wall covering.*

ABOVE RIGHT *This well-worn leather armchair with elegant turned and carved legs has a book stand attached to allow heavy books to be rested at a comfortable height and angle.*

169

Beds

Four-poster beds, which had been unfashionable in the late eighteenth and early nineteenth centuries, became popular again in the early Victorian period, along with canopies and hangings that matched the window curtains. But with the growing concern about health and hygiene in the latter part of the nineteenth century, heavy bed drapery, which could harbour dust, began to be seen as a health hazard. Four-posters fell into disfavour, half-testers became the preferred style once more and a lighter look emerged. Wooden beds, too, were deemed hazardous to health, and metal bedsteads began to replace rosewood and mahogany beds. Cast iron was usually painted, but brass beds were preferred. The top and end rails were decorated with brass scrolls, animals and flowers in urns. Later, mother-of-pearl and porcelain were also being used.

RIGHT *This elegant four-poster bed has a chintz fabric for the outer curtains and is lined in a contrasting plain red. Rather than using fringes to edge the canopy, a double frill has been attached which gives added fullness. The fur throw is a nice contemporary touch.*

170

Glossary

Acanthus: Widely used classical motif representing jagged leaves of acanthus plant.

Applied decoration: Ornament completed in advance and attached to furniture, fireplace, wall or other surface.

Architrave: MOULDING around doors or windows.

Ball-and-claw foot: Carved furniture foot shaped like a claw (often an eagle's) gripping a ball; mostly used with CABRIOLE LEG.

Balloon-back chair: Chair with unupholstered back in which uprights meet top rail in a continuous curve; shaped like a hot-air balloon and popular in Victorian times.

Baluster: Banister, or small post, supporting a handrail.

Balustrade: Series of BALUSTERS forming a low wall or barrier such as a staircase.

Boat-bed: Bed with scrolled ends, also known as sleigh bed or by French term *lit-bateau or lit en bateau*; popular in Empire and Regency styles.

Bolection moulding: MOULDING used to cover joint between two members with different surface levels. Usually of S-section, it projects beyond both surfaces.

Cabriole leg: Furniture leg in gently curving S-shape; characteristic of Queen Anne and Chippendale furniture.

Caryatid: Draped female figure of classical origin used as decorative support.

Chair rail: Wall MOULDING at height of chair backs; also known as dado rail, it often runs along top of DADO but can be used without dado.

Chaise longue: Upholstered 'long chair', with seat elongated for reclining. Also known as a daybed.

Chinoiserie: Romanticized version of Oriental style.

Coffered ceiling: Ceiling divided into coffers, or compartments, by plaster mouldings or exposed beams; coffers often decorated with carved, moulded or painted decoration.

Column: Vertical member, circular in section. Component of classical architecture.

Commode: Low chest of drawers, often with bowed front.

Composition: Amalgam used for APPLIED DECORATION.

Console table: Table attached to wall and supported by scroll-shaped brackets (consoles) or legs. Often used beneath a PIER GLASS.

Cornice: Decorative MOULDING that covers joint between wall and ceiling (sometimes known as crown moulding).

Couch: *CHAISE LONGUE* with two ends but no back, or with one end and a half-width back.

Cove ceiling: Ceiling with a smooth, concave transition to wall.

Crewelwork: Embroidery in WORSTED yarn on plain linen or wool.

Crockets: Leaf carving projecting at regular intervals from sloping edge; used with PINNACLES in GOTHIC(K) decoration.

Dado: Lower portion of interior wall between level of CHAIR RAIL and skirting board (baseboard).

Daybed: See *CHAISE LONGUE*.

Dentil mouldings: Decorative moulding made up of rectangular, tooth-like blocks at regular intervals.

Egg-and-dart moulding: Decorative moulding made up of alternating ovals and arrowheads.

En suite: All in the same fabric.

Entablature: Section of a fireplace or cabinet corresponding to entablature in classical architecture, which is the upper part of a building, supported by columns.

Fauteuil: Upholstered French armchair with open sides.

Faux paint finish: Decorative paint finish that simulates marble, wood, tortoiseshell, etc.

Festoon: See SWAG.

Field: Main part of wall, below PICTURE RAIL and FRIEZE, and above CHAIR RAIL and DADO.

Fillet: Thin border hiding joint between stretched fabric or wallpaper and wall. Made from cord, wood, metal, papier mâché or COMPOSITION.

Finial: Carved, moulded or cast ornament at end of a curtain rod, bedpost, etc.

Flock paper: Wallpaper resembling velvet or damask, made by covering glue with powdered fibres to create raised pattern.

Fluting: Parallel vertical grooves on a cylindrical surface, such as a COLUMN or PILASTER.

Frieze: portion of wall below CORNICE and above FIELD and PICTURE RAIL.

Full tester: Four-poster bed, with canopy ('tester') extending entire length.

Gothic(k): Medieval style of architecture and design characterized by pointed arches, vertical lines, complex window tracery, QUATREFOILS, PINNACLES and CROCKETS. Revivals in 18th and 19th centuries known as Gothic, Gothick and Gothic Revival respectively.

Greek key: Classical fretwork pattern consisting of continuous lines at right angles, resembling a maze; often used as a border.

Half-tester: Bed with two posts at head but none at foot, and with shortened canopy suspended from ceiling.

Inlay: Small pieces of ivory, mother-of-pearl, horn, metal or different-coloured woods, set into wooden surface to decorate it.

Jambs: Vertical sides of fireplace, arch or doorway.

Japanning: Imitation LACQUERWARE decorated with CHINOISERIE motifs.

Jib door: Concealed door that is flush with wall and is usually decorated to match it.

Lacquerware: Wooden furniture and accessories with a hard, high-gloss finish from many layers of lacquer. Usually left black or dyed red; could be carved or decorated with INLAY.

Lath-and-plaster ceiling: Ceiling in which beams and joists are plastered over, using network of thin slips of wood as supporting base for flat plaster.

Limed (pickled) finish: Originally, finish resulting from treating wood such as oak or elm with slaked lime to prevent woodworm, or 'pickling' it with harsh chemicals that stripped away the colour. Today, a similar effect is achieved by rubbing white paint or white wax into the grain and rubbing off the excess.

Lit-bateau or **lit en bateau:** See BOAT-BED.

Marquetry: Decorative veneer made up of shaped pieces of wood, bone, ivory, etc, applied to furniture to create a figurative scene or naturalistic pattern. Geometrical patterns are known as parquetry.

Medallion: Circular or oval ornament, often containing other motifs, applied to plaster and other surfaces.

Moiré: Watered finish creating wavelike pattern on fabric such as silk.

Moulding: Shaped ornamental strips of wood, plaster or stone applied to surface as decoration or to conceal joints.

Newel post: Structural post at head and foot of stairs.

Ombras: Wood or metal hold-back, over which curtain is draped.

Ormolu: Mercury-gilded bronze, or any gilt-bronze decoration applied to furniture as mounts.

Overdoor: Ornamental structure over a door such as a wooden PEDIMENT or a plasterwork panel.

Overmantel: Ornamental structure over a mantelpiece.

Parquet floor: Wood flooring in which thin strips of different-coloured hardwoods are laid in geometric pattern.

Parquetry: See MARQUETRY.

Passementerie: Decorative trimmings such as fringes, braids and tassels.

Pedestal: Square block beneath statue, vase, COLUMN or PILASTER; decorated with MOULDINGS at top, unlike PLINTH.

Pediment: Classical triangular shape used above doors, windows and fireplaces, and on cabinet furniture such as bookcases. A 'broken pediment' has a gap at the apex.

Pelmet: Stiffened band of fabric across the top of a window or around a bed canopy. An unstiffened fabric pelmet is also called a valance.

Piano nobile: 'Noble' or principal floor, either the raised ground floor or the floor above entrance level.

Pickled finish: See LIMED (PICKLED) FINISH.

Picture rail: Moulding between FRIEZE and FIELD on wall.

Pier glass: Tall, narrow mirror hung on the wall ('pier') between two windows, over a pier table such as a CONSOLE TABLE.

Pilaster: Semicircular or rectangular column against wall, often flanking doorway, cabinet door or fireplace opening, and used decoratively rather than for support.

Pinnacles: Small conical turrets used with CROCKETS in GOTHIC(K) decoration.

Plinth: Square block beneath cabinet furniture, statue, vase, COLUMN or PILASTER; no mouldings at top, unlike PEDESTAL.

Porphyry: Hard, fine-grained rock that is dark red or purple (or grey or green) and flecked with white.

Quatrefoil: Four-lobed leaf motif, often found in GOTHIC(K) decoration.

Reeding: Parallel narrow mouldings, used as chair and table leg decoration.

Rush light: Candle made by dipping rush in tallow.

Sabre leg: Furniture leg with outward curve resembling sabre, usually with REEDING; popular during Regency and Empire periods.

Scagliola: Composite imitation marble made from polished plaster and marble chips.

Scrolls: Curved decoration, such as C-shaped and S-shaped scrolls found on mirror and Rococo picture frames, bureaux and chairs.

Strapwork: Ornament resembling interlaced straps, applied or carved, in wood, stone or plaster.

Stucco: In interiors, fine plaster incorporating marble dust rather than animal hair, and used on surface of walls and in decoration.

Swag: Classical decoration depicting draped garland of fruit and flowers or loop of fabric; also known as festoon.

Swag and tails (cascades): Draped window treatment, with horizontally draped fabric swag in centre, and tails (cascades) hanging at either side.

Tall-boy: Small chest of drawers on top of larger one.

Toile: Cotton fabric printed with pictorial scenes in single colour, from late 18th century. Toiles de Jouy, from France, are best known but toiles were also produced in England and Ireland at same time.

Tripartite division of walls: Neoclassical theory that an interior wall should be divided into three main sections, with proportions corresponding to those of main sections of classical Order: ENTABLATURE, COLUMN and PEDESTAL.

Trompe l'oeil: French term for 'fool the eye', referring to paint techniques that create illusion of three dimensions.

Turkeywork: English imitations of rugs from Turkey, Persia and Far East.

Wainscot: Panelling applied to DADO.

Worsted: Twisted yarn or thread spun from combed wool, or fabric woven from it.

Acknowledgments

The author would like to thank Cindy Richards and Georgina Harris and all those at CICO books who have assisted with this project. She would also like to thank Charles Miers and also those at Rizzoli for their continued support.

The author and publishers would like to thank the photographers and designers responsible for the beautiful images in this book. All photographs, except those courtesy and copyright © Ianthe Ruthven on pages 55, 68, 76 and 108, are courtesy of the Interior Archive and copyright © the photographers, Simon Upton, Fritz von der Schulenburg, Luke White and Andrew Wood.

Page 1: photog. Fritz von der Schulenburg–des. John Russell.
Page 2: photog. Fritz von der Schulenburg.
Page 3: photog. Simon Upton.
Page 5: photog. Fritz von der Schulenburg–des. John Russell.
Page 6: photog. Simon Upton.
Page 7: photog. Fritz von der Schulenburg.
Page 8: photog. Fritz von der Schulenburg–des. Adelheid von der Schulenburg.
Page 9: photog. Fritz von der Schulenburg–des. Jensen.
Page 10: photog. Fritz von der Schulenburg.
Page 11: photog. Fritz von der Schulenburg.
Page 12: photog. Simon Upton–des. David Hare.
Page 13: photog. Fritz von der Schulenburg.
Page 14: photog. Fritz von der Schulenburg.
Page 15: photog. Fritz von der Schulenburg.
Page 16: photog. Fritz von der Schulenburg.
Page 17: photog. Fritz von der Schulenburg.
Page 18: photog. Fritz von der Schulenburg.
Page 19: photog. Simon Upton–des. Alidad.
Page 20-21: photog. Fritz von der Schulenburg.
Page 22: photog. Fritz von der Schulenburg.
Page 23: photog. Fritz von der Schulenburg.
Page 24, left: photog. Fritz von der Schulenburg–des. Janet Fitch;
right: photog. Fritz von der Schulenburg.
Page 25: photog. Fritz von der Schulenburg–des. Christopher Gibbs.
Page 26: photog. Simon Upton–des. Bolsa.
Page 27, left: photog. Simon Upton;
right: photog. Simon Upton–des. Alidad.
Page 28: photog. Simon Upton–des. Lars Sjoeberg.
Page 29: photog. Fritz von der Schulenburg–des. Karl Lagerfeld.
Page 30: photog. Fritz von der Schulenburg.
Page 31, left: photog. Simon Upton–des. David Hare;
right: photog. Simon Upton–des. Patrice Butler.
Page 32: photog. Fritz von der Schulenburg.
Page 33, left: photog. Fritz von der Schulenburg;
right: photog. Fritz von der Schulenburg–des. Karl Lagerfeld.

Page 34: photog. Simon Upton–des. Alidad.
Page 35: photog. Simon Upton–des. Alidad.
Page 36: photog. Fritz von der Schulenburg.
Page 37: photog. Fritz von der Schulenburg.
Page 38: photog. Fritz von der Schulenburg–des. Bill Blass.
Page 39: photog. Fritz von der Schulenburg.
Page 40: photog. Fritz von der Schulenburg.
Page 41: photog. Simon Upton.
Page 42: photog. Simon Upton–des. The English Stamp Co.
Page 43, top: photog. Fritz von der Schulenburg;
bottom: photog. Fritz von der Schulenburg.
Page 44: photog. Fritz von der Schulenburg.
Page 45: photog. Luke White.
Page 46: photog. Fritz von der Schulenburg.
Page 47: photog. Fritz von der Schulenburg.
Page 48: photog. Fritz von der Schulenburg.
Page 49, left: photog. Fritz von der Schulenburg–des. Bill Blass;
right: photog. Fritz von der Schulenburg–des. Alec Cobb.
Page 50: photog. Fritz von der Schulenburg–des. Willa Elphinstone.
Page 51: photog. Fritz von der Schulenburg.
Page 52, left: photog. Simon Upton–des. David Hare;
right: photog. Fritz von der Schulenburg.
Page 53: photog. Fritz von der Schulenburg–des. Willa Elphinstone.
Page 54: photog. Simon Upton–des. Bolsa.
Page 56: photog. Simon Upton–des. David Hare.
Page 57: photog. Fritz von der Schulenburg.
Page 58: photog. Simon Upton–des. Burke.
Page 59: photog. Simon Upton.
Page 60: photog. Fritz von der Schulenburg.
Page 61, left: Fritz von der Schulenburg–des. Jill de Brand;
right: photog. Fritz von der Schulenburg.
Page 62: photog. Fritz von der Schulenburg.
Page 63: photog. Simon Upton–des. David Hare.
Page 64, left: photog. Fritz von der Schulenburg;
right: photog. Fritz von der Schulenburg.
Page 65: photog. Fritz von der Schulenburg–des. Jill de Brand.

Page 66: photog. Fritz von der Schulenburg.
Page 67, left: photog. Fritz von der Schulenburg;
right: Fritz von der Schulenburg.
Page 69: photog. Fritz von der Schulenburg–des. Bill Blass.
Page 70: photog. Fritz von der Schulenburg–des. Bill Blass.
Page 71: photog. Fritz von der Schulenburg.
Page 72: photog. Simon Upton–arch. Randolph Martz.
Page 73: photog. Fritz von der Schulenburg.
Page 74: photog. Fritz von der Schulenburg–des. Bill Blass.
Page 75: photog. Fritz von der Schulenburg.
Page 77: photog. Fritz von der Schulenburg.
Page 78: photog. Fritz von der Schulenburg–des. Bill Blass.
Page 79: photog. Fritz von der Schulenburg–des. Bill Blass.
Page 80: photog. Fritz von der Schulenburg.
Page 81: photog. Fritz von der Schulenburg.
Page 82: photog. Fritz von der Schulenburg–des. John Russell.
Page 83: photog. Fritz von der Schulenburg.
Page 84: photog. Fritz von der Schulenburg.
Page 85: photog. Fritz von der Schulenburg–des. John Russell.
Page 86: photog. Fritz von der Schulenburg.
Page 87: photog. Fritz von der Schulenburg.
Page 88: photog. Fritz von der Schulenburg.
Page 89, top: photog. Simon Upton–des. Marie Anne von Kantzow;
bottom: photog. Fritz von der Schulenburg.
Page 90: photog. Fritz von der Schulenburg.
Page 91: photog. Fritz von der Schulenburg.
Page 92: photog. Fritz von der Schulenburg.
Page 93: photog. Fritz von der Schulenburg.
Page 94, left: photog. Fritz von der Schulenburg–des. Karl Lagerfeld;
right: photog. Fritz von der Schulenburg–des. David Bennett.
Page 95: photog. Fritz von der Schulenburg.
Page 96: photog. Fritz von der Schulenburg.
Page 97: photog. Fritz von der Schulenburg.
Page 98: photog. Fritz von der Schulenburg–des. Bill Blass.
Page 99: photog. Fritz von der Schulenburg.
Page 100: photog. Fritz von der Schulenburg–des. Bill Blass.
Page 101: photog. Fritz von der Schulenburg.
Page 102: photog. Fritz von der Schulenburg.
Page 103: photog. Fritz von der Schulenburg.
Page 104: photog. Fritz von der Schulenburg.
Page 105: photog. Fritz von der Schulenburg.
Page 106: photog. Fritz von der Schulenburg–des. Willa Elphinstone.
Page 107: photog. Fritz von der Schulenburg.
Page 109: photog. Fritz von der Schulenburg.
Page 110: photog. Simon Upton–des. Alidad.
Page 111: photog. Fritz von der Schulenburg.
Page 112: photog. Fritz von der Schulenburg–des. Alec Cobb.
Page 113: photog. Fritz von der Schulenburg.
Page 114, left: photog. Fritz von der Schulenburg;
right: Fritz von der Schulenburg–des. Willa Elphinstone.
Page 115: photog. Fritz von der Schulenburg.
Page 116: photog. Simon Upton–des. David Hare.
Page 117, left: photog. Simon Upton–des. David Hare;
right: photog. Simon Upton–des. David Hare.
Page 118: photog. Fritz von der Schulenburg.
Page 119, left: photog. Fritz von der Schulenburg;
right: photog. Fritz von der Schulenburg.
Page 120: photog. Fritz von der Schulenburg–des. Jean Louis Germain.
Page 121: photog. Fritz von der Schulenburg.
Page 122: photog. Simon Upton–des. Lars Sjoeberg.
Page 123: photog. Luke White–des. John Coote.
Page 124: photog. Fritz von der Schulenburg–des. Janet Fitch.
Page 125: photog. Fritz von der Schulenburg–des. Janet Fitch.
Page 126-127: photog. Fritz von der Schulenburg–des. Christopher Vane Percy.
Page 128: photog. Luke White–des. John Coote.
Page 129: photog. Luke White–des. John Coote.
Page 130: photog. Fritz von der Schulenburg–des. Christopher Vane Percy.
Page 131: photog. Fritz von der Schulenburg–des. John Fowler.
Page 132: photog. Simon Upton–des. Tim Gosling.
Page 133: photog. Simon Upton–des. Tim Gosling.
Page 134: photog. Fritz von der Schulenburg.
Page 135: photog. Fritz von der Schulenburg.
Page 136: photog. Simon Upton–des. David Hare.
Page 137: photog. Fritz von der Schulenburg.
Page 138: photog. Fritz von der Schulenburg–des. Christopher Hodsoll.
Page 139: photog. Fritz von der Schulenburg–des. Christopher Hodsoll.
Page 140: photog. Fritz von der Schulenburg–des. Christopher Vane Percy.
Page 141: photog. Fritz von der Schulenburg–des. Christopher Vane Percy.
Page 142, top: photog. Simon Upton–des. Marie Anne von Kantzow;
bottom: photog. Simon Upton–des. Burke.
Page 143, top: photog. Andrew Wood–des. Henrietta Spencer-Churchill;
bottom: photog. Fritz von der Schulenburg–des. John Fowler.
Page 144: photog. Fritz von der Schulenburg–des. David Hicks.
Page 145: photog. Fritz von der Schulenburg.
Page 146: photog. Fritz von der Schulenburg.
Page 147: photog. Fritz von der Schulenburg.
Page 148: photog. Simon Upton–des. Alidad.
Page 149: photog. Fritz von der Schulenburg.
Page 150: photog. Fritz von der Schulenburg.
Page 151: photog. Simon Upton–des. Alidad.
Page 152: photog. Fritz von der Schulenburg.
Page 153: top: photog. Simon Upton;
bottom: photog. Fritz von der Schulenburg.
Page 154: photog. Simon Upton–des. Bolsa.
Page 155: photog. Fritz von der Schulenburg–des. Jill de Brand.
Page 156: photog. Fritz von der Schulenburg.
Page 157: photog. Simon Upton.
Page 158: photog. Fritz von der Schulenburg.
Page 159: photog. Simon Upton.
Page 160: photog. Fritz von der Schulenburg.
Page 161: photog. Fritz von der Schulenburg.
Page 162: photog. Simon Upton–des. David Hare.
Page 163, left: photog. Andrew Wood–des. Henrietta Spencer-Churchill;
right: photog. Fritz von der Schulenburg–des Janet Fitch.
Page 164: photog. Fritz von der Schulenburg–des. Christopher Gibbs.
Page 165: photog. Fritz von der Schulenburg.
Page 166: photog. Fritz von der Schulenburg.
Page 167: photog. Fritz von der Schulenburg.
Page 168: photog. Fritz von der Schulenburg–des. Christopher Hodsoll.
Page 169, left: photog. Fritz von der Schulenburg;
right: Simon Upton.
Page 170: photog. Fritz von der Schulenburg.
Page 171: photog. Simon Upton–des. Annabel Astor.

Index

Adam style 38, 88, 91, 94
American Empire style
    98–119

Baroque style 10–35, 37, 56,
    69, 75, 158
beds, bed hangings:
    American Empire 99, 113,
    114, 117
    Baroque 28, 31, 64
    Federal 97
    Georgian 64
    Regency 144, 147
    Victorian 170
blinds see curtains, blinds
bookcases, libraries:
    American Empire 111
    Baroque 27
    Georgian 37, 61
    Regency 135, 141
    Victorian 166

carpets see rugs, carpets
ceilings:
    American Empire 99, 105
    Baroque 20, 75
    Colonial 74–75
    Federal 88
    Georgian 50
    Regency 122, 127–129
    Victorian 155
'Chinese taste', chinoiserie
    38, 61, 64, 121,142
classical motifs 55, 56, 62,
    83, 91, 94, 100, 107, 113,
    119, 121
classical style see Neoclassical
    style
Colonial style 68–81, 83
curtains, blinds:
    American Empire 99, 106,
    107
    Baroque 24, 31
    Colonial 78
    Federal 93, 97
    Georgian 52
    Regency 122, 144
    Victorian 159, 160, 163,
    170

doors:
    American Empire 106
    Baroque 22
    Colonial 69
    Federal 91
    Georgian 37
    Regency 133, 144

Empire style see American
    Empire style and French
    Empire style

Federal style 82–97, 108, 112
fireplaces:
    American Empire
    108,119
    Baroque 22
    Colonial 69, 72, 77, 83
    Federal 84, 91
    Georgian 37, 55
    Regency 135, 144
    Victorian 157, 158, 159,
    168
    floors:
    Baroque 12,
    Colonial 69, 72
    Federal 84, 86
    Georgian 40–43
    Regency 122
    Victorian 152
French Empire style 99, 100,
    107, 112, 114, 119, 129,
    130, 144
    furniture:
    American Empire 99, 106,
    112–113, 117, 119
    Baroque 27
    Colonial 69, 81
    Federal 94, 112
    Georgian 61–62
    Queen Anne 27
    Regency 122, 141, 142
    Shaker 70, 81
    Victorian 149, 150,
    168–169

Georgian style 36–67, 83,
    93, 158
Gothic style 38, 55, 149,
    152, 158, 163, 166, 168
Gothic(k) motifs 62
'Gothick taste' 38, 61, 62,
    121, 133
Greek Revival style 100,
    105, 106, 112, 133

halls:
    Baroque 14
    Federal 86
    Georgian 40–43, 67
    Victorian 152

libraries see bookcases,
    libraries
lighting:
    American Empire 99

Baroque 32–33
Colonial 70
Federal 84
Georgian 67
Regency
Victorian

mirrors:
    American Empire 108,
    113, 119
    Baroque 22, 33, 56
    Federal 84
    Georgian 56
    Regency 136
    Victorian 157, 169

Neoclassical style 38, 49, 50,
    52, 55, 62, 83, 91, 93,
    149, 163

Oriental style 38, 97
Ornamentation, ornaments:
    American Empire 99, 102,
    105, 107, 108, 108, 113,
    114, 119
    Baroque 11, 14, 19, 20,
    22, 27, 32–33
    Colonial 70, 75, 77, 81
    Federal 83, 86, 88, 91,
    94
    Georgian 37, 47, 49, 50,
    52, 55, 56, 61, 62, 67
    Regency 121, 124, 125,
    127, 133, 135, 136
    Victorian 150, 157, 170

Palladian style 37, 38, 47, 55,
    56, 61, 69, 86
paintings, pictures:
    American Empire 102,
    108, 119
    Baroque 20, 22
    Colonial 70, 77
    Federal 88
    Georgian 59
    Regency 128
    Victorian 158, 165
panelling:
    American Empire 106
    Baroque 11, 17, 19, 22
    Colonial 69, 72, 77
    Georgian 47, 49
    Regency 127, 133

Queen Anne style 11–12, 24,
    69

Regency style 99, 102,
    120–147
Rococo style 37–38, 52, 55,
    56, 61, 64, 75, 149, 158
rugs, carpets:
    American Empire 99, 105,
    119
    Baroque 12
    Colonial 72
    Federal 84
    Georgian 41–42
    Regency 122, 125
    Victorian 152

Shaker style 70, 81
stairs
    Baroque 14
    Colonial 69
    Federal 86
    Georgian 44
    Regency 124

textiles, tapestries:
    American Empire 99, 102,
    105, 107, 113, 114 117,
    119
    Baroque 19, 24, 31, 35
    Colonial 70, 78, 84
    Federal 93, 97
    Georgian 49, 52, 62, 64
    Regency 121, 122, 127,
    129, 130, 142, 144
    Victorian 149, 160, 163

Victorian style 148–171

walls:
    American Empire 99, 102,
    105, 119
    Baroque 17, 19
    Colonial 70, 72
    Federal 88
    Georgian 37, 47–49
    Queen Anne 17
    Regency 127–129
    Victorian 155–163
windows:
    American Empire 99,
    106
    Baroque 24
    Colonial 78
    Federal 93
    Georgian 52
    Queen Anne 52
    Regency 130
    Victorian 150, 160